Official Compilation of TRIVIA and FACTS of Jamaica and its People 1962-2012

Compiled by: Nina Hart

First published in the USA by Six Hearts Publishing

First USA Edition–2013

TEST YOUR JAMAICA IQ

Copyright by Nina Hart 2013

Published in the Unites States of America

Cover Design: Ashley Wright
Cover: Daniell Washington of The Big Blue and You (www.bigblueandyou)
Cover Girl's Wardrobe: Don Salmon of Rastawear Collection, Venice, CA
Cover Photograph: Alexander H. Davis
Graphic Design: Huntley Burgher
Photographs by: Huntley Burgher, Jamaica Tourist Board & Jeaneane (Jen) Swaby

Published by Six Hearts Publishing
Davie, Florida
www.sixheartspublishing.com

January 2013

ISBN: 978-0-9899172-0-9
Library of Congress Control Number: 2013949342

Information for this Publication was sourced in part from:
www.visitjamaica.com (Jamaica Tourist Board web site)
www.jis.gov.jm   www.gleanerarchives.com, (Gleaner Company)
National Library of Jamaica, The National Weekly
and The Worldwide Web

Disclaimer

The information provided in this book was obtained from a variety of research sources, including the Internet, newspapers, magazines, books, and personal interviews. We must emphasize that Six Hearts Publishing is not the originator of most of the content of this book, but we have made a stringent attempt to ensure that the information published is accurate and factual. We disclaim any responsibility for any inaccurate information that might have been overlooked by our editorial staff.

Nina Hart, Publisher

CONTENTS

Devon House in Kingston. Photograph courtesy of the Jamaica Tourist Board

Dedication

This book is dedicated to every Jamaican on the planet.

It is intended to be used as a tool to educate and inform Jamaicans

Of our rich heritage, especially the 3rd and 4th generations of Jamaicans.

Acknowledgements:

I would like to express a hearty 'Thank You,' to our friends at the Jamaica Tourist Board, namely; Ms. Sharille Pink and Ms. Essie Gardner for their support of this publication. We would not have been able to compile as much information if it were not for the contribution of the Jamaica Tourist Board.

Thanks Jen for readily agreeing to share your prized photographs of Jamaica to enhance this publication. Jamaicans across the world will appreciate your beautiful photographs and we invite everyone to take a peak at more of your treasured shots at www.ThruJensEyes.com.

Special thanks to my friend and supporter Dr. Garth Rose, for always believing in me and providing whatever information that was required to make this publication possible. I appreciate you and thank you for being my sounding board.

Thanks and appreciation to my Publication Partner, Huntley Burgher who did not hesitate when I approached him with the idea of this celebrated publication.

We owe a gigantic 'Thank You' to 'Team Jamaica,' who proudly represented Jamaica in the 2012 London Olympics; once again Jamaica was paraded in front of the world. Usain Bolt, Shelly Ann Fraser and the rest of the team, you all did a phenomenal job!

Thank you coaches, you were the force behind the 2012 London Olympics.

Thank you to everyone who contributed to making this book posible. It has truly been a team effort and my sincerest appreciation to all.

"Together Everyone Achieves More"

Charitable Contributions:

Part proceeds from the sale of each book will be donated to 'Clint O'Neil Needy Kids of Jamaica' and also 'Free Me Inc,' an organization committed to help free victims of domestic violence anywhere in the world, but this initiative will focus on women in Jamaica. (www.freemeinc.org).

PREP FOR THE TEST

(The information listed below covers the period from 1962-2012, this section will give clues to the Trivia questions throughout this book).

1962

February 27: New Jamaican Constitution is ratified by the Jamaican Parliament.

April: The JLP wins General Election, which would make Sir Alexander Bustamante the new nation's first Prime Minister.

July: Sir Kenneth Blackburn was appointed by her Majesty Queen Elizabeth II on the recommendation of the then Premier to be the first Governor General of Independent Jamaica.

Aug: At midnight August 5, the British flag was lowered and the Jamaican flag hoisted, to symbolize Jamaica becoming an independent nation within the British Commonwealth. A ceremony was held at the newly constructed National Stadium.

August 6 is celebrated as the first Independence Day with celebrations, including street dancing, across the country.

October: Clifford Campbell, a JLP legislator, and teacher, is appointed as the first Jamaican to serve as the nation's governor general.

1963

March: The Hon Donald Sangster is appointed Deputy Prime Minister.

November: Carol Joan Crawford is chosen "Miss World 1963," A first for a Jamaican.

November: Marcus Garvey's body is returned to Jamaica, and he is declared the first National Hero. His body is interred in the Marcus Garvey Memorial in King George VI Memorial Park, (Heroes' Park) in Kingston.

1965

January: Jamaica becomes a member of the United Nations Human Rights Commission for the first time.

June: Dr. Martin Luther King Jr. visits Jamaica and address the valedictory service of graduating students of the University of the West Indies. During the visit he is presented with the Keys to the City of Kingston at a civil reception at the National Stadium.

October: The 100th anniversary of the Morant Bay Rebellion is celebrated. It's announced that in honor of Bogle, a son of St. Thomas, the town of Morant Bay would be raised to mayoral status. A monument honoring Paul Bogle and George William Gordon as National Heroes is dedicated at the King George VI Memorial Park.

1966

April: His Imperial Majesty (H.I.M.), Haile Selassie, Emperor of Ethiopia, arrives amidst a great reception, in Jamaica for a three-day state visit. H.I.M. addresses the Jamaican Parliament and at a special ceremony at the University of the West Indies receives the honorary degree of Doctor of Laws.

August: Jamaica hosts the 8th British Empire and Commonwealth Games.

September: The Rt. Rev. Percival W. Gibson, C.B.E., D.D., the first Jamaican to be elevated to the office of Anglican Bishop of Jamaica, retires.

1967

February: The JLP wins a second term in General Elections.

Succeeding Sir Alexander Bustamante, The Hon. Donald Sangster is sworn in as the second Prime Minister of Jamaica by then Governor-General Sir Clifford Campbell.

April 11: The Hon Donald Sangster dies in Canada. Her Majesty the Queen dubs him Knight Commander of the Royal Victorian Order. The Hon Hugh Lawson Shearer is elected by the JLP to succeed him and is sworn in as Jamaica's third Prime Minister.

1968

August: Jamaica officially becomes a member of CARIFTA, the forerunner to the Caribbean Community (CARICOM).

December 10: The Marcus Garvey Prize for Human Rights (£5000) is awarded posthumously to Dr. Martin Luther King Jr.

1969

February: Norman Washington Manley resigns as Leader of the Opposition and the House of Representatives. His son, Michael, is elected leader of the People's National Party (PNP).

September 2: Norman Washington Manley dies. Five days later he is buried in the National Shrine of the King George VI Memorial Park.

September: Jamaica decimalizes its currency; changing from pounds, shillings and pence to the Jamaican Dollar.

October 20: National Heroes' Day is established as an annual holiday.

1970

May: The statue of the Rt. Excellent Sir Alexander Bustamante, Jamaica's only living National Hero, is unveiled by Lady Bustamante during a ceremony at Victoria Park.

1971

October: National Heroes' Day is celebrated with a military parade and the first investiture of purely Jamaican awards at Up Park Camp. The Rt. Excellent Sir Alexander Bustamante receives his Order of National Hero.

1972

February: The PNP led by Michael Manley scores a massive victory over Hugh Shearer and the JLP, and Manley is sworn in as the new prime minister.

Jamaican cricketer Lawrence Rowe, set a record as the first batsman to score centuries in both innings on his test debut 214 and 100 not out.

April: The Centenary celebrations of Kingston as the capital of Jamaica opens with a Divine Service at Kingston Parish Church.

June: The Hon. Michael Manley weds Beverly Anderson, the second Prime Minister to get married while in office.

1973

June: The Hon. Florizel A. Glasspole, C.D., is sworn in as Governor-General succeeding Sir Clifford Campbell.

May: Prime Minister Manley in his budget presentation at Gordon House announces free education–no tuition fees to be paid for secondary schools and the University of the West Indies.

1974

The Manley government passes social reform legislation including the Equal Rights for Equal Pay Act, Status of Children Act, Maternity Leave with Pay Act, Minimum Wage Act, Termination and Redundancy Pay Act, Holiday with Pay Act.

1975

October: Nanny of the Maroons and Samuel Sharpe were declared National Heroes bringing the number of Jamaican National Heroes to seven. Charles Square in Montego Bay was re-named Sam Sharpe Square in honor of the National hero.

May: The Commonwealth Heads of Government Meeting is held in Kingston, attended by prime minister and presidents of the nations that comprise the British Commonwealth.

1976

August: Sprinter Donald Quarrie wins a gold medal in the 200 meters, and silver at the Summer Olympics in Montreal, Canada.

November: Cindy Breakspeare becomes the second Jamaican woman to be win the Miss World title.

1977

August 6: Jamaica's first prime minister and surviving National Hero, Sir Alexander Bustamante, dies at age 93.

October: Cuban leader Fidel Castro pays a six-day official visit to Jamaica as a guest of the government.

1979

January: Jamaica is elected to serve on the United Nations Security Council for the first time.

1980

June: 1980, a plot was discovered by the Jamaica Defence Force (JDF) to overthrow the Government. Twenty-four Jamaica Defence Force personnel and three civilians were detained. All those tried were eventually freed.

October: The JLP wins the General Elections and Edward Seaga becomes prime minister.

1981

May: Robert Nesta Marley dies in Miami, Florida from cancer. A state funeral was held for him at the National Arena, Kingston and earlier in April he was invested with the Order of Merit (O.M.).

August 21: Jamaica is chosen as the Headquarters of the International Seabed Authority.

1982

February: Lady Gladys Bustamante is invested with the Order of Jamaica.

The President of the United States Ronald Reagan and his wife makes a state visit to Jamaica.

1983

February: Her Majesty Queen Elizabeth II, and His Royal Highness the Duke of Edinburgh pay a state visit to Jamaica. Her Majesty officially opens the Interim Headquarters of the International Seabed Authority in Kingston.

1984

Jamaica celebrates Jamaica 21 representing 21 years of independence.

August: The centenary of the birth of National Hero the Rt. Excellent Alexander Bustamante is celebrated. (He was born in 1884).

August: Jamaica participates in (LAO) Los Angeles Olympics, winning 1 silver and 2 bronze medals.

1985

February: Reggae band, Black Uhuru is the first recipient of the Grammy award for Reggae.

Canasol, a new drug developed from marijuana (ganja), is introduced by Professor Manley West and Dr. Albert Lockhart for the treatment of glaucoma. Both were awarded the Order of Merit in 1987.

1986

The College of Arts, Science and Technology awards its first bachelor's degrees in education, home economics and engineering.

1987

In local government elections, the JLP loses control of the majority of the parish council to the PNP.

February: The Hon. Edna Manley, O.M., one of Jamaica's foremost artists, widow of National Hero, the Right Excellent Norman Manley, mother of former Prime Minister Michael Manley, and Dr. Douglas Manley dies. She is buried beside her husband at the National Heroes' Park.

August: The Centenary of the birth of National Hero the Rt. Excellent Marcus Garvey is celebrated.

1988

February: Jamaica made history in the Winter Olympics, when a Jamaican bobsled team entered the bobsledding competition at the Olympics in Calgary, Alberta, Canada.

August 1: A $50 note with the portrait of National Hero the Rt. Excellent Sam Sharpe is issued for the first time.

August: Jamaica participates in the Seoul, South Korea, Olympics, winning 2 silver medals.

Hurricane Gilbert struck Jamaica with excessive force.

1989

The PNP wins General Election and Michael Manley is returned as prime minister.

1990

August: Sir Florizel Glasspole, Governor General since 1973, retires and is succeeded by Sir Howard Cooke.

1991

July: Nelson Mandela, South Africa President, visits Jamaica with his wife, Winnie, to a tumultuous welcome. Mr. Mandela is awarded an honorary degree by the University of the West Indies.

September: Sir Clifford Campbell, the first native Governor-General of Jamaica dies at age 90.

1992

March: The Rt. Hon. Michael Manley, PNP Leader and Prime Minister, resigns in March for health reasons. Percival James Patterson is elected by the PNP to replace him and is sworn in as new Prime Minister.

In the Barcelona, Spain, Olympics, Jamaica wins 3 silver and 1 bronze medal.

1993

March: P.J. Patterson leads the PNP in victory in General Elections, his first victory as leader of the PNP.

August: Pope John Paul II pays an official visit to Jamaica.

Lisa Hanna wins the Miss World crown in South Africa, the third Jamaican to win the Miss World title.

The Movie *Cool Runnings* is released based on the story of the Jamaican bobsled teams in the Calgary Winter Olympics.

1996

August: Jamaican hurdler, Deon Hemmings wins the gold medal in the 400 meters hurdle at the Summer Olympics in Atlanta, USA. The Jamaican team wins 1 gold, 3 silver and 2 bronze medals.

1997

March 6: The Rt. Hon Michael Manley dies after a long illness. His funeral is attended by several Caribbean and international heads of state and political figures. He is interred at National Heroes' Park.

December: PNP wins a third term in General Elections.

1998

Jamaica's national football team creates Soccer World Cup history when the national team, the Reggae Boyz, qualifies for the World Cup in France. The team defeats Japan in the first round, but did not advance.

1999

April: Violent protests erupt against a 30% increase in fuel prices.

July: Government orders the army to patrol the streets of Kingston following a massive increase in crime.

2000

January: Jamaica is elected to serve on the United Nations Security Council for the second time.

August: Jamaica wins 4 silver and 5 bronze medals at the Summer Olympics in Melbourne, Australia.

2002

February: Jamaica is one of three Commonwealth countries visited by Her Majesty Queen Elizabeth II in celebration of her Golden Jubilee.

October: Prime Minister PJ Patterson's People's National Party wins general elections, for fourth successive term, and PJ his third successive term as prime minister.

2004

March: Ousted former Haitian president Jean-Bertrand Aristide takes asylum in Jamaica on the agreement of the Jamaican government.

August: At the Summer Olympics in Athens, Greek, Jamaican sprinter Veronica Campbell wins gold in the 200 meters, as did the women 4 x 100 meters relay team. The Jamaican team won 2 gold, 1 silver and 2 bronze medals.

September: Hurricane Ivan, one of the biggest hits in the island, destroying thousands of homes and properties.

2005

January: Former Prime Minister Edward Scaga retires as leader of the JLP.

February: Bruce Golding is elected as head of the JLP.

September: Prime Minister PJ Patterson announces he will retire as leader of the PNP and prime minister by April 2006.

2006

February: Portia Simpson Miller is elected as leader of the PNP and Member of Parliament.

March: Portia Simpson Miller becomes Jamaica's first female prime minister.

2007

September: The JLP led by Bruce Golding defeats the PNP in general elections, and Golding is sworn in as prime minister.

2008

Jamaica has its best ever Olympic performance at the Summer Games in Beijing, China, winning 6 Gold, 3 Silver and 2 Bronze Medals. 21-year-old Usain Bolt emerges as the star of the games, winning gold in the 100, 200 meters and 4 x 100 meters relay, breaking the world record each time.

2010

May-June–Dozens killed in security operations to arrest alleged drug lord Christopher "Dudus" Coke. He is extradited to the US.

June: Coke extradited to the US.

2011

October: Prime Minister Bruce Golding resigns as head of the Jamaican Labor Party and prime minister.

October: Andrew Holness is selected by the JLP executives to be the new party leader and the youngest Jamaican prime minister ever. He was born in 1972.

December: Portia Simpson Miller leads the PNP to general elections victory over the JLP.

2012

January: Portia Simpson Miller is sworn in for the second time as Jamaica's prime minister.

August: Jamaica commemorates its 5oth anniversary of political independence.

Reference: yush.com /Countdown to Independence. Jamaica Journal, 46 (1982) p. 21-24.

NATIONAL HEROES OF JAMAICA:

Paul Bogle: Baptist Deacon and a Jamaican rebel who led the Morant Bay Rebellion.

Sir Alexander Bustamante: Jamaican politician and labour leader who became the first Prime Minister after Jamaica's Independence.

Marcus Mosiah Garvey: He was a journalist, entrepreneur, publisher, Black Nationalist, and founder of the 'Universal Negro Improvement Association and The African Communities League.'

George William Gordon: Born to a white planter and a slave he was a self taught Jamaican businessman and politician.

Norman Washington Manley: He was a well known statesman and one of the leading lawyers of Jamaica in the 1920s. He was the Founder of the People's National Party.

Nanny of the Maroons: She lived about 250 years ago. A well-recognized leader of the Maroons in the 18th century, she was known to free over 800 slaves over a span of 50 years

Samuel 'Sam' Sharp: Though a well-educated man he was a slave throughout his life. Highly respected by other slaves, he was a good preacher and leader.

Who Am I?
Politics

JAMAICAN POLITICS TRIVIA 1

I was born on December 5, 1947.

1962–I successfully sat the Cambridge Examination before I was 15 years old.

1963–I transferred to Jamaica College to pursue Religious Knowledge and was also chosen to represent the school as Head Boy.

1966–I enrolled in the University of the West Indies where I studied Economics. I graduated three years later with a B.Sc. Degree in Economics.

1967–While still at university I suspended my studies due to changes in the constituency boundaries which resulted in a political crisis for my father. At 20 years old, I took charge of my father's campaign and won the seat by a small margin of 878.

1968–I was elected Vice Chairman of the Jamaica Labour Party.

1969–I was selected as the candidate for West St. Catherine. I was also elected to the Central Executive of the Jamaica Labour Party and was one of the founders of the youth arm "Young Jamaica."

1972–At 24 years old, I was the youngest Member of Parliament.

1974–Was the year I was elected General Secretary of the Jamaica Labour Party.

1995–I tendered my resignation to the Jamaica Labour Party and I founded the National Democratic Movement (NDM).

2002–After intensive negotiations I reentered the Jamaica Labour Party.

2005–I was elected Chairman of the Party and in April of the same year elected Member of Parliament for the constituency of West Kingston as well as Leader of the Opposition.

2007–I was sworn in as Prime Minister of Jamaica as what was said to be the closest election in the history of Jamaica.

2011–I tendered my resignation as Prime Minister of Jamaica.

JAMAICAN POLITICS TRIVIA 2

I was born in Kingston on September 25, 1909, I was the son of a Methodist minister and my mother was Florence. I was educated at Buff Bay Elementary School in Portland, Central Branch Primary School in Kingston and Wolmer's Boys School. I graduated after four years with both Junior and Senior Cambridge Examinations.

My first job was in the Civil Service with the Registrar of Titles Office, it was during this time I had a strong desire to help improve the lot of my fellowman. Often times, the working conditions and low salaries of plantation laborers made my heart pound with sympathy.

As my interest in the trade union movement grew, I married the beautiful, Ina Josephine Kinlocke and the union produced one daughter, Sara Lou Mena.

There was a strong emphasis on education during my time and I presided twice over the Education portfolio, from 1957 to 1962 and again from 1972 to 1973.

June 27, 1973, I became the second Jamaican to be appointed Governor-General of Jamaica. I remained in office for 17 eventful years, the longest period for a Governor-General to date.

I saw to the construction of the Ministry of Education headquarters at National Heroes' Circle.

I saw to the College of Arts, Science and Technology (CAST), now the University of Technology (UTech), to operate as a multifaceted tertiary institution.

I saw to the Free Education Policy of the 1970s, and the In-service Teachers Education Trust (ISTET) which allowed teachers to upgrade their qualification on the job.

Declaration of Spanish as the second official language of Jamaica.

I was the recipient of a long and impressive list of national and international awards and honors, culminating in the Order of the Nation (O.N.), Jamaica's second highest honor after The Order of National Hero.

In 1981 I was knighted by Her Majesty Queen Elizabeth II, receiving the Grand Cross of the Most Distinguished Order of St Micheal and St George (GCMG) in a private function at Buckingham Palace.

I retired from the office in 1990. Away from the glare of public life and the glamour of hosting royalties and heads of state, I spent my last days working on my memoirs.

I died on November 25, 2005 at the age of 91.

JAMAICAN POLITICS TRIVIA 3

I was born on October 15, 1915.

1962–1967, became a Senator.

1967–1980, I was appointed member of the House of Representatives.

1972–1980, I was elected Minister of Government.

1980–I was awarded a Special Plaque by the Commonwealth Parliamentary Association.

1982–1991, I continued a successful career in the Insurance Industry/American Life.

1989–1991, I became President of the Senate.

1991–I was appointed Governor General on August 1, 1991; I was the 3rd to fill that position since Jamaica gained Independence in 1962.

1991–Her Majesty, Queen Elizabeth, bestowed on me 'The Knighthood (GCMG).'

1991–I was awarded the 'Order of the Nation.'

1991–I received the Mico College Gold Medal Award for outstanding service as I was a full time teacher prior to entering the political arena.

2006–I resigned office February 16, 2006.

I have been married to Lady Sylvia for over six decades and we're parents to three children, two sons and a daughter.

JAMAICAN POLITICS TRIVIA 4

I was born July 22, 1972.

1994–Prior to entering representational politics, I worked as the Executive Director of one of Jamaica's oldest non-government organizations (NGOs), the Voluntary Organization for Uplifting Children (VOUCH) and in that capacity, led extensive social work in several inner city communities of Kingston.

1996–I joined the Premium Group of Companies and functioned as a special assistant to then Leader of the Opposition, the Most Hon. Edward Seaga. In my capacity as personal assistant, I was assigned the responsibility of developing poverty reduction and social investment policies for the Jamaica Labor Party (JLP).

1997–At the age of 25 I was first elected to the House of Representatives to represent my home district of West Central St. Andrew as a Member of Parliament.

1999-2000–I served as Opposition Spokesperson on Land and Development.

2002–I switched portfolio to Housing.

2005–I was asked by the new leader of the JLP, Bruce Golding, to take on the topical issue of education.

2007–I was sworn in as the Minister of Education after the JLP won general election.

2011–I was sworn in as Jamaica's ninth Prime Minister and also the youngest to take the office of Prime Minister of Jamaica.

2011–December 2011, General Elections were called and I was replaced by the Opposition Leader, the Hon. Portia Simpson, now Prime Minister of Jamaica.

I am married to Juliet, a chartered accountant and businesswoman and we have two boys.

JAMAICAN POLITICS TRIVIA 5

I was born on December 10, 1924 to a father who was a Rhodes scholar, decorated World War I hero, and the most distinguished legal advocate in the history of Jamaica. My mother was an internationally recognized sculptor and patron of the arts. I attended Jamaica College; I was a writer for the weekly newspaper Public Opinion. I volunteered for service in the Royal Canadian Air Force in 1943 while at McGill University and at the end of the war studied politics, philosophy, and economics at the London School of Economics. Upon graduation I worked as a freelance journalist with the British Broadcasting Service when I accepted the invitation to be associate editor of Public Opinion.

Three years later I quit Public Opinion to work full time with the National Worker's Union. Prior to 1962 I was elected Island supervisor and first vice president of the National Workers Union, and in 1962, I was elected president of the Caribbean Bauxite and Mineworkers Union. Before my formal entry into politics I had the reputation of being the foremost union organizer in the Caribbean–an energetic, fearless, dynamic, and gifted leader.

In the general elections of 1967 I won the seat in the House of Representatives for the constituency of Central Kingston, later reclassified as East Central Kingston. I was elected leader of the People's National Party in 1969, I led the party to victory in 1972.

My first two terms as prime minister created great controversy and projected the country into international headlines. In an effort to implement my brand of "democratic socialism" I sought to drastically restructure the politics and economy of Jamaica through far-reaching legislation. On the positive side, over 40,000 new housing units were built, free education was made available for all students, new hospitals were established and the infant mortality rate was cut in half. However, the Jamaican economy took a nosedive due to several factors. The price of oil increased nearly ten-fold, the government's purchase of most of the sugar estates resulted in them becoming unproductive white elephants; and many business and professional people, feared that that the country was heading towards communism. As a result, unemployment skyrocketed to thirty percent by 1980 and despite the critics I developed close ties with Cuba.

We lost the 1980 election to the Jamaica Labor Party (JLP). After nine years in opposition, I returned to power in 1989, inheriting an even more bankrupt economy. By then I had recanted much of my earlier radicalism. My government presented itself as pro-business and advocated privatization policies, although still maintaining cautious links with Fidel Castro. In 1990 I was diagnosed with cancer, and on March 16th I announced that I was stepping down as prime minister owing to declining health. In spite of my illness, I led the Commonwealth Observer Mission to oversee the historic 1994 elections in South Africa, which ended apartheid. I died of prostate cancer March 7th, 1997 after having served my country for over 40 years.

JAMAICAN POLITICS TRIVIA 6

I was born in 1935; I was the son of a farmer and a primary school teacher.

1953–I graduated from Calabar High School.

1955–I began political activity at the University of the West Indies, where I was one of the founders of the Political Club this position brought me into contact with several prominent members of the People's National Party (PNP).I made my first appearance as a speaker on a political platform in the election campaign for the candidate for Western Hanover. After that, political involvement took precedence over every other interest in my life.

1958–I graduated from the University of the West Indies (UWI) at Mona, with a B.A. (Honours) in English.

1963–I graduated from the London School of Economics, where I studied Law; I was awarded the Leverhume Scholarship and the Sir Hughes Parry prize for Excellence in the Law of Contracts. I was called to the Bar at Middle Temple in 1963 and also admitted to the Jamaican Bar in that year.

1969–I was elected Vice-President of the Peoples National Party.

1972–I was appointed as Minister of Industry, Trade and Tourism.

1978-1980–I served as Deputy Prime Minister and Minister of Foreign Affairs and Foreign Trade.

1983–I served as Party Chairman for the Peoples National Party.

1989-1990–I was the Deputy Prime Minister and Minister of Development, Planning and Production.

1990-1991–I served as Deputy Prime Minister and Minister of Finance and Planning.

1992–I was appointed Prime Minister of Jamaica, following my election as President of the PNP, on the retirement of former Prime Minister, the late Michael Manley.

1993–I was returned to office following the national elections of 1993 during that year I created the National Commission on Science and Technology and was the first to directly link Jamaica's science and technology initiatives with the nation's industrial policy.

2002–I have the distinction of being the first Prime Minister to be sworn in for a fourth consecutive term of office, after I led the PNP to victory in the elections of October 2002.

JAMAICAN POLITICS TRIVIA 7

I was born on May 28, 1930. I was educated at Wolmer's Boys' School in Jamaica and later graduated from Harvard University.

1965–I married Elizabeth "Mitsy" Constantine; we have two sons and a daughter.

My political career began when I was 29 years old–I was the youngest member appointed to the Legislative Council, which established the framework for national independence in August 1962.

1960's–I transformed the country's then worst slum, "Back-O-Wall", into a modern, low-income residential community, renamed Tivoli Gardens.

1962–I was elected Member of Parliament for Western Kingston and I held that seat for 40 consecutive years.

1967–Following General Elections, I became Minister of Finance and Planning.

1974–I became the Leader of the Jamaica Labour Party (JLP) and the Parliamentary Opposition until the General Elections of October 30, 1980.

1980-1989–I served as Prime Minister of Jamaica.

1980's–Under my Administration the Income and Corporate Tax System was comprehensively reformed and modernized to make it more equitable and efficient.

1981–I created the highly successful Jamaica National Investment Promotion Ltd. (now JAMPRO), as a one-stop investment organization to promote local and overseas investment in Jamaica.

1981–Queen Elizabeth II appointed me as a member of her Majesty's Privy Council.

1983–Pan American Development Foundation Inter-American, Man of the Year award.

1996–I married Carla Vendryes, we have a daughter.

JAMAICAN POLITICS TRIVIA 8

I was born on April 24, 1941 and hails from the Parish of Hanover.

1972-1974–I lectured in History at the University of the West Indies, Mona.

1982-1884–I served as Professor at the State University of New York (SUNY), I taught History and American Studies.

1994–I returned to the Caribbean in 1994 and was appointed Deputy Secretary General of CARICOM two years later.

1996–I became Pro-Vice Chancellor/Principal of UWI, Mona.

2003–I was appointed Chairman of the Caribbean Examination Council. I also served as Chairman of the Board of Directors of Mona Institute of Business.

2006–I became Jamaica's fifth Governor General on February 15, 2006.

I have also been affiliated with several associations. I served as Consultant, to some local and international organizations. I have published several books, articles and papers. My publications include:

The Caribbean Community: Beyond Survival

Caribbean Imperatives: Regional Governance

Contending with Destiny: The Caribbean in the 21st Century

Integrate or Perish: Perspectives of leaders of the integration movement, 1963-1969.

I am married to Rheima and we have one daughter.

JAMAICAN POLITICS TRIVIA 9

I was born on December 12, 1945 in the rural community of Wood Hall, St. Catherine.

1974–My political career began when I was asked to represent Trench Town in the Municipal Elections.

1976–I became Member of Parliament for South West St. Andrew.

1977–Parliamentary Secretary in the Ministry of Local Government and in the Office of the Prime Minister.

1978–I was Vice President for the People's National Party.

1989–Minister of Labor, Social Security and Sport.

2000–Minister of Tourism and Sport.

2002–Minister of Local Government Community Development and Sport.

2002–The Union Institute of Miami conferred upon me the degree of Honorary Doctor of Humane Letters. I was the first graduate to receive the Institute's Honorary Degree.

2006–History was made in Jamaica when I was sworn in as Jamaica's first female Prime Minister.

My accomplishments include reform to the Overseas Farm workers program through the Overseas Recruitment Centre for Farm Workers.

High on my agenda is the employment of youth and women.

I am an avid supporter of Jamaican athletes and I'd often attend events dressed in the National colors.

It was under my leadership, as Sports Minister that the Indoor Sports Facility at the National Stadium was built and the Sports Development Foundation established.

2012–The people of Jamaica spoke and once more I am back in office as Prime Minister of Jamaica.

I am married to Errald.

JAMAICAN POLITICS TRIVIA 10

I was born February 7, 1951 in the farming community of Fruitful Vale, Portland; I am the fourth of five children of Ferdinand and Christina. After completing my GCE examinations in 1968 by private study, I joined the staff of the school as a pre-trained teacher at the age of 17. Two years later, I enrolled in the Moneague Teacher's College.

1976-1978–I was the principal of Robins Bay All-Age. In 1978 I became Principal of the Hillside Primary School in St. Mary, which had an enrollment four times the size of Robins Bay.

As a devout Seven Day Adventist I have felt a call on my life since I was 11 years old to serve as a full time pastor. In 1980 I entered Andrews University in Michigan where I attained a Bachelor's degree in History and Religion before pursuing a Master's degree in Systematic Theology. I returned to Jamaica in 1986 and was assigned as a pastoral intern to various churches in Spanish Town and May Pen.

1990-1993–I served as Director of Education and Family Life of the West Indies Union of Seventh Day Adventists.

1996-1998–I returned to Andrews University and earned my Ph.D degree in Educational Administration and Supervision. Upon my return to Jamaica I was elected President of the Central Jamaica Conference of Seventh Day Adventists.

2000–I was elected President of the West Indies Union of Seventh Day Adventists with overall responsibility for the Seventh Day Adventist churches and related organizations in Jamaica, Bahamas and the Cayman Islands.

2005–I was re-elected President. I was Chairman of the Board of Governors of Northern Caribbean University. I was Chairman of the Board of Directors for Andrews Memorial Hospital, Adventist Development and Relief Agency, Book and Nutrition Centre Ltd. and West Indies Union Investment Management Ltd.

2006–The Jamaican government conferred on me the rank of Commander of the Order of Distinction (CD) for service in education, religion, and social work.

2009–Queen Elizabeth the second, appointed me as Knight Grand Cross of the Most Distinguished Order of St Michael and St George. On February 26, 2009 I was appointed Governor General of Jamaica. I am the sixth person to hold this position since independence in 1962.

JAMAICAN POLITICS TRIVIA 11

I was born February 24, 1884 to an Irish Roman Catholic planter and my mother was of mixed race. After travelling the world, including working as a policeman in Cuba and as a dietician in a New York City hospital, I returned to Jamaica in 1932 and became a leader of the struggle against colonial rule. During the 1938 labour rebellion I was quickly identified as the spokesman for striking workers.

I was imprisoned for subversive activities in 1940. However, the anti-colonial effort resulted in the granting of universal suffrage to Jamaica. I was released from prison in 1943 and founded the Jamaica Labour Party.

1962–I married Gladys Maud Longbridge, my personal secretary.

Jamaica was granted independence in 1962 and I served as the first Prime Minister to an independent Jamaica until 1967.

1963–I was made a member of the Private Council, I also I received an honorary degree from the American University, Fairfield, Connecticut.

1965–I withdrew from active participation in public life, and real power was held by my deputy, Donald Sangster.

1966–The honorary degree of Doctor of Laws 'honoris causa' of the University of the West Indies was conferred on me.

1966–I was awarded the National Order of Knight Grand Cross. I was also awarded the Distinguished Order of the Brilliant Star with special Grand Cordon by the Government of the Republic of China.

1967–I retired from office.

1968–The Jamaican House of Representatives and the Senate paid tribute to me. Also my Foundation was launched simultaneously in four countries, as a permanent and lasting memory of my services to Jamaica.

1969–I became a National Hero and my statue was erected at South Parade, my picture appears on the Jamaican dollar bill.

1977–I died at 93 years old.

JAMAICAN POLITICS TRIVIA 12

I was born on August 27, 1975 to parents Rene and Dorothy and grew up in Retreat, St. Mary. My father was a farmer and my mother was a hairdresser.

As a young girl I worked as a volunteer with the World Hunger Project and the JAMAL programs in Jamaica alerting people to the global status of hunger, starvation and the local plight of adult illiteracy. I also worked in conjunction with UNICEF to spearhead the Jamaican candlelight vigils to launch the International Convention on the Rights of the Child. I continued my community service and blazed a trail as Head Girl at Queen's High School. I became television co-host for one of Jamaica's most popular television programs, *Rappin'* and became one of the youngest United Nations Goodwill Ambassadors ever to be appointed by the United Nations Development Program in Jamaica.

1993–I won the title of Miss World representing Jamaica, making me the 3rd Jamaican to win this prestigious title.

1998–I acted in the film *How Stella Got Her Groove Back,* as Abby.

1998-2000–I achieved my Bachelor of Arts and Master of Arts degrees in communications from the University of the West Indies. During my tenure, I raised funds and built the Computer Facility for the Faculty of Arts and the Humanities, accessed several thousands of dollars in scholarships and grants for UWI students, trained over 2000 Jamaican children in character development through my workshop and taught women in the skills training programs in Jones Town.

2007–As a member of the People's National Party, I became one of the youngest women to be elected to the Jamaican Parliament after winning the seat for South East St Ann. In addition to my duties as constituency representative I served as opposition spokesperson on Information, Youth and Culture, up to December 2011.

2009–I was ranked number one on the Chester Francis-Jackson top 10 best dressed women.

2011–On the December 29, the People's National Party won the general elections.

2012–I was elected Minister of Youth and Culture in the Jamaican Cabinet.

JAMAICAN POLITICS TRIVIA 13

I was born on May 18, 1923 in the village of Martha Brae just outside of Falmouth, Trelawny. My parents were James and Esther.

I attended the Falmouth Primary school and later St. Simon's College, a privately owned high school in Kingston. When I entered the workforce there was intense political and labor turmoil in Jamaica as the leaders of both parties were engaged in the struggle to reshape and redefine the Jamaican society.

Prior to 1962, I held various positions as Trade Unionist/Politician.

In 1963, I presented a proposal to the United Nations that 1968 to be designated as "Human Rights Year." This proposal was accepted by the United Nations General Assembly.

In the 1967 general elections, I won the Clarendon seat which had been held by Sir Alexander Bustamante before his retirement from active politics.

In the new Government, I was appointed Minister of External Affairs on February 27, 1967.

On the passing of Sir Donald Sangster, I was chosen to be Prime Minister of Jamaica. I was sworn in on April 11, 1967.

On January 6, 1969 I was appointed by Her Majesty Queen Elizabeth II as Member of the Privy Council of England.

During my tenure as Prime Minister, Jamaica attained its highest ever gross domestic product (GDP) per capita–US$2,300–based on rapid growth in agriculture, mining and tourism.

I also started a system of major highways, the first being the Kingston to Spanish Town Highway, and laid the plans for other by-pass routes. I had a special interest in education and my goal was to provide a sound education for every child in Jamaica.

I was awarded the Doctor of Laws, honoris causa, by Howard University in 1968 and the University of the West Indies (UWI) in 1994.

I died at my home in Kingston on July 5, 2004 at the age of 81, leaving my wonderful wife, three sons and five daughters.

JAMAICAN POLITICS TRIVIA 14

I was born October 26, 1911; I was the son of W. B. and Elizabeth. I was educated at Munro College and was admitted to practice as a solicitor in Jamaica in 1937.

My political career started when I was only twenty-one when I campaigned and won a seat in the St. Elizabeth Parochial Board. I became Vice-Chairman of my Parochial Board and later, Chairman.

Prior to 1962 I filled various roles in the political arena and in 1962 I was reappointed to the House of Representatives. That very year when the JLP was returned to office I was appointed Minister of Finance and subsequently Deputy Prime Minister.

I was appointed to act as Prime Minister, Minister of External Affairs and Minister of Defense in January 1965 as a result of the illness of the Prime Minister, the Rt. Hon. Sir Alexander Bustamante. While acting, I retained the post of Minister of Finance.

I was Leader of Jamaica's delegations to the Commonwealth Economic Consultative Council Conferences in 1963-1966. I led Jamaica's delegation to the World Bank and International Monetary Fund meetings in Washington (1963-1966). I had been a Governor of the World Bank and IMF since 1963.

I was a member of Jamaica's delegation to the Heads of Commonwealth Caribbean conference in Port-of-Spain Trinidad 1963, and Kingston Jamaica in 1964. I led the delegation to these conferences in Georgetown, Guyana in 1965 and in Bridgetown Barbados in 1966. I also led Jamaica's delegation to the Canada-Commonwealth Caribbean Countries in Ottawa in July 1966.

I accompanied Sir Alexander Bustamante to the Commonwealth Prime Ministers' Conference in London in 1962 and I attended this conference as Sir Alexander's representative in 1964. I attended as Acting Prime Minister, the conferences in London in 1965, Lagos in 1966.

When Sir Alexander Bustamante resigned, I was appointed Prime Minister on February 22, 1967 retaining at the same time the posts of Minister of Finance and Minister of Defense. I became Jamaica's second Prime Minister, the shortest term Prime Minister, in the history of Jamaica. I succeeded Sir Alexander Bustamante on February 23, 1967 and died on April 11, 1967 in Montreal, Canada. My face appears on the Jamaican one hundred dollar bill and an airport in Jamaica is named after me.

JAMAICAN POLITICS TRIVIA 15

I was born on born October 20, 1913, I attended Wolmer's Girls School and from there I started a business career. I have always been known to be a strong, outspoken Jamaican.

I was affectionately known as Madame. I first made my name as a beautician, succeeding in business at a time in Jamaica when very few women were involved in commerce.

I entered politics when I was twenty-seven at which time both parties were in their infancy stage.

I became the first woman to chair a national political party, the Jamaica Labor party, holding that position for 12 years during a period of growing self-government.

I was elected a member of the House of Representatives, and later, I was appointed minister of health and social welfare. As a politician I always put people first and would sometimes go to extremes to demonstrate that I wanted the best for them.

Due to my blatant honesty I had a disagreement with the Jamaica Labor Party which forced me to leave that party and represent the opposition, the Peoples National Party.

1971-1972 I became Deputy Mayor of Kingston, and during 1972 I became a Member of Parliament and Minister of local government in Michael Manley's administration. I am the first Jamaican politician to hold ministerial posts under both political parties.

I left Jamaica for the US to study at the Abyssinian School of Cosmetic Chemistry, on my return to Jamaica I became the co-founder of the 'Leon School of Beauty Culture' with my husband, Arthur. I pioneered a line of locally made beauty products, providing an alternative when most women had to buy from abroad.

I resigned from politics in the early 80s, but remained active in the island's civic and business life. Some of my interests included membership of the Jamaica Manufacturers Association, the Lay Magistrates Association and the National Council for the Aged.

On August 16, 1999 I was murdered in my home in Jamaica at the age of 85, survived by my daughter Gloria.

Who Am I?

Sports

Shelly-Ann Fraser-Pryce is a world champion sprinter and Olympic gold medalist

JAMAICAN SPORTS TRIVIA 1

I was born on the 30th of October 1962 to parents Joan and Eric–I grew up on cricket, hearing the sound of bat hitting ball, evening after evening.

1983–I was selected as a member of the Jamaica youth team in where I contributed towards the team's victories.

1984–85 I became a member of The West Indies Cricket team for 18 years.

1988–I took a unique Hat Trick in the first test of the 1988-89 series against Australia in Brisbane with last ball of first innings and first two balls of my first spell in the second innings.

1994–I was appointed West Indies captain for a tour of India and New Zealand.

1995–I had my test careers best bowling performance of 7-37 in the second test against New Zealand in Wellington.

I became the second Jamaican and the seventh West Indian bowler to take 200 wickets in test cricket when I trapped Bast Ali, leg before wicket in the second innings of the second test against Pakistan at Kensington Oval.

1998–I became West Indies leading Wicket-taker in tests when I passed Malcolm Marshall's Mark of 376 wickets in my first test against South Africa in Johannesburg.

1999–I was the first West Indian and only third bowler in test history, after Kapil Dev (434) and Sir Richard Hadlee (431), to take 400 test wickets.

2000 - 2001–West Indies played against South Africa at Kingston in 2000- 01 thus setting the world record for the most test wickets taken. Retired from international cricket April 2001.

2005 - June 20th–The road where Melbourne Cricket Club is located was renamed after me (was previously known as Derrymore road).

I participated in 131 test matches, the most by any West Indian.

I have two children, my son's life ambition is to become the best bowler in the world and I also have a daughter.

JAMAICAN SPORTS TRIVIA 2

I was born on August 21, 1986 in Sherwood Content, a small town in Trelawny, Jamaica, and grew up with my parents and two siblings.

I spent my childhood years playing cricket and football in the street with my brother. "When I was young, I didn't really think about anything other than sports."

In primary school I became the school's fastest runner over 100 meters.

Former Prime Minister P.J. Patterson recognized my talent and arranged for me to move to Kingston, along with Jermaine Gonzales, so I could train with the Jamaica Amateur Athletic Association (JAAA) at the University of Technology, Jamaica.

2002–2003, At the Junior World Championship I had a chance to prove my credentials on the world stage. I won the 200 meters, in a time of 20.61 making me the youngest world-junior gold medalist. I won four gold medals at the 2003 CARIFTA Games.

2007–I participated in the 2007 World Championships in Osaka, Japan, winning a silver medal.

2008 Beijing National Stadium–I was the first man to win three sprinting events at a single Olympics since Carl Lewis in 1984 and also the first man to set world records in all three events. This made me the first man to hold both the 100 and 200 meter world and Olympic titles at the same time. I donated US$50,000 to the children of the Sichuan province of China to help those harmed by the 2008 Sichuan earthquake.

2009–My record breaking margin over 100 meters is the highest since the start of digital time measurements. After a series of victories at the Berlin World Championship, on the last day of the Championship, governing Mayor of Berlin, Klaus Wowereit, presented me with a 12-foot high section of the Berlin Wall in a small ceremony, saying I had shown that "one can tear down walls that had been considered insurmountable."

2010–I signed a lucrative publishing deal with Harper Collins for an autobiography, which was negotiated by Chris Nathaniel of NVA Management. I am a Jamaican Sprinter, a five-time World and three-time Olympic Gold Medalist.

2012 London Olympics–Proudly celebrated Jamaica's 50 years of Independence by bringing home 3 gold medals and the first man to ever retain Olympic 100 and 200 meter titles. I am a Champion!

JAMAICAN SPORTS TRIVIA 3

I was born on 25 February 1951 in Kingston Jamaica.

I am a former Jamaican athlete, one of the world's top sprinters during the 1970s.

1970–Commonwealth Games, I won gold medals in both the 100 and 200 meter races.

1971–Pan American Games in Cali. My time in the 200 meters was a hand-timed 19.8 seconds.

1974–Commonwealth Games in Christchurch; I repeated my 1970 performance by grabbing the 100 and 200 meter titles, becoming the first athlete to retain the title in either event.

1976–After winning the AAA's 100/200 titles, I could finally compete at the Olympics without injuries.

1984–Los Angeles Olympics, I won a fourth Olympic medal with the Jamaican relay team, which finished second behind the United States.

I competed in five Olympic games and has received recognition both on and off the field.

With 15 years of athletic consulting with an emphasis on athlete and federation relationships, motivation of individual athletes, sprint/running clinics, organizing international track meets and personal training programs. In October 2006 I signed a contract with the Chinese Athletics Association to work as a consultant in the preparations for the 2008 Summer Olympics in Beijing.

My statue is proudly positioned at the entrance to Jamaica's National Stadium.

JAMAICAN SPORTS TRIVIA 4

I was born December 27, 1986 to a mother who was once a runner, therefore, I believed sprinting was in my blood. I attended Wolmers' Girls School, Kingston Jamaica and represented my school in many athletic occasions.

2005–Bacolet, Tobago–I was a participant in the women's 4 x 100 relay, Gold Medal recipients.

2007–Helped Jamaica qualify for the 4 x 100 final at the 2007 World Championships in Osaka, Japan, my team was placed second in the final and we took home silver medals.

2008 Olympics in Beijing–I was a 100 meters Gold Medalist; I sprinted to victory in 10.78 seconds. This victory made me the first Jamaican woman to win Olympic Gold in the 100 meters.

In 2009, I won the 100 meters title at the 2009 World Championships, held in Berlin, Germany, becoming the second female sprinter in history to simultaneously hold both Olympic and world 100 meters titles.

2010–I was named as the first UNICEF National Goodwill Ambassador for Jamaica on February 22 and on February 23; I was named Grace Goodwill Ambassador for Peace for 2010 in a partnership with Grace Foods and not-for-profit Organization PALS (Peace and Love in Society).

2012 London Olympics–I became the first woman since American Gail Devers in 1992 and 1996 to win back-to-back 100 meters titles at the Olympic Games. I am ranked fourth on the list of the fastest 100 meters female sprinters of all time, with a personal best of 10.70 seconds, set in Kingston, Jamaica in 2012.

I attended the University of Technology in Kingston, Jamaica.

JAMAICAN SPORTS TRIVIA 5

I was born May 10, 1960, to Hubert and Joan in Cold Spring, Hanover, Jamaica. I was introduced to athletics by my mother, who bought me a manual on track and field.

In my early school years in the 1970s, I frequently competed barefoot in local races. I was inspired by Donald Quarrie from the 1976 Summer Olympics in Montreal.

My athletics career took off when I migrated to the U.S., and attended the University of Nebraska in 1979, where I joined the track team. I represented Jamaica in the 1979 Pan American Games, winning a bronze medal in the 200 meters.

So far, I have the longest career as a top level international sprinter, which has not yet concluded as I anchored the Slovenian 4 x 100 relay at the 2010 European Athletics Championships at the age of 50.

Because of my achievements and longevity in Track and Field, I have earned the name the "Queen of the Track."

1980 Moscow Games–I became the first female English speaking Caribbean athlete to win an Olympic medal. Back in Jamaica, I was awarded an Officer of the Order of Nation, and the Order of Distinction for 'services in the field of sport.'

1982 Commonwealth Games–I won a gold medal in the 200 meters, and a silver medal in the 100 meters. Nearly a decade later, in the 1990 Commonwealth Games, I won gold in both events. I was named Ambassador of Jamaica after my gold medal win in the 1993 world championships.

1979-1997, I have been named Jamaican Sportswoman of the year 15 times over an 18 year span.

Throughout my career, I have won nine Olympic medals, the most by any woman in track and field history. I have had seven Olympic appearances from 1980 to 2004, the most by any Track & Field athlete.

I won 14 World Championship medals between 1983 to 1997—more than any other athlete, male or female.

I was appointed an Ambassador at Large by the Jamaican government in 1993. After some controversy pertaining to my Athletic Career as a Jamaican, I made the decision to move to Slovenia in 1998. In 2002 I became a Slovenian citizen, and now reside in Ljubljana, where I represent my new country in international events.

At 50+, I have no plans in hanging up my spikes.

JAMAICAN SPORTS TRIVIA 6

I was born August 1, 1954 in Norwich, Port Antonio. In my early years I had a vision from God and by the time I was twenty-one, I entered the world of professional boxing.

1976–I represented Jamaica in the Summer Olympics in Montreal, Canada as a heavyweight boxer, despite having had only 11 prior amateur bouts. My lack of experience was plainly evident as I lost to the eventual silver medalist, Mircea Simon of Romania. After the Olympics I migrated to Canada and fought professionally out of Montreal and Halifax.

1979–I won my first 11 fights (10 by knockout) before suffering my first pro loss to another rising contender, Bernardo Mercado, on April 3.

1981–I lost a 15-round unanimous decision to Larry Holmes on April 11. Then later that year I fought Muhammad Ali, winning a 10-round unanimous decision in Nassau, Bahamas on December 11. Ali was 39-year-old and this was the final fight of his career.

1982 - 1984, I beat undefeated prospect, Greg Page, then in 1084 relocated to Miramar, Florida and signed with promoter Don King.

1986–I won the WBC world heavyweight title by upsetting Pinklon Thomas with an easy unanimous decision. However, my reign as champion would be brief, as I was knocked down twice in the second round by 20-year-old Mike Tyson. I got up from the first knockdown, but after the second I fell to the canvas three times while trying to get up, prompting referee Mills Lane to stop the fight, which gave me a TKO loss.

Again, I made boxing history—this time by being the man who Tyson defeated for his first heavyweight title, symbolically bridging the eras of Ali and Tyson, as fight commentator Barry Tompkins said after the knockout: "And we have a new era in boxing!"

In 1991, I went to the UWFI in Japan to fight Nobuhiko Takada in a "boxer vs. wrestler" bout but my contender claimed victory by default when I exited the ring.

My last appearance in the ring was in 2000 against Canadian journeyman Shane Sutcliffe, winning a 12-round unanimous decision. Afterwards, a CAT scan revealed a blood clot in my brain and my boxing license was revoked. My final professional record was 49 wins (33 by knockout), 12 losses, and 1 draw. After I retired I ran into problems with the law and was deported back to Jamaica. On October 28, 2006 I was murdered at a church in the little town where I was born by my nephew and an alleged accomplice.

JAMAICAN SPORTS TRIVIA 7

I was born February 1957 and I am currently a retired Jamaican track cyclist.

1975–I competed in the Pan American Games in Mexico City and won a silver medal in the 1000 meters time trial.

1979–Pan American Games in San Juan, I won a silver medal in the 1000 meters time trial.

1980–Summer Olympics in Moscow I won a bronze medal in 1000 meters time trial, becoming the first (and still the only) Jamaican to win an Olympic medal in another sport other than athletics (track and field). I was timed at 1:05.241 seconds and was beaten by Aleksandr Panfilov (1:04.845) of Uzbekistan, and Lothar Thoms of Germany (1:02.955). I retired after the 1980 Olympics and went back to school.

1984–After being out of the competition for two years, I came back and with a broken wrist finished 6th while US finished about 9th.

In addition, I won bronze (1983) at the Pan Am Games and 2 gold medals at the CAC (Central American and Caribbean) Games (1978) in record time. The record was broken in the 1990s. I also won a bronze at the 1978 Commonwealth Games in Canada.

After the 1984 Olympics I moved to Miami and I was coaching some athletes between 1986 - 1989. Some of them were master's level athletes who went on to place in the World Masters Championships. One of them was Jan Jardine, Hillary Jardine's (of motor racing fame) son.

I moved up to Atlanta in 1991 and ran a team called Atlanta Velo. From there we started a team in 1992 and in 1995 our team took a medal in every single event on the velodrome at the U.S. national championships, and then we placed second at the U.S. Olympic Trials, which was unheard of for a club team.

At that time, Chris Carmichael, who is Lance Armstrong's coach, wanted to come and see what we were doing in Atlanta.

Every good success has to start with a plan and as a teenager I started with a plan and I owe a lot of my success to John Hall (father of Michael Hall, Carreras Foundation chairman).

JAMAICAN SPORTS TRIVIA 8

In 1966, the Davis Cup team consisting of Lumsden and myself, defeated Venezuela by 3-2, the first time that a Jamaican team had ever won a Davis Cup tie. In the following Davis Cup tie against the United States at the St Andrew Club in Kingston, Lumsden and I scored a famous victory on May 21, 1966, when we won the doubles match against the top-ranked American duo of Arthur Ashe and Charlie Pasarell, winning in five sets 6-4, 7-9, 14-12, 4-6, 6-4. This was the first time that the Commonwealth Caribbean had won a Davis Cup match against the United States. Although the United States won the tie by 4-1, this doubles victory by Lumsden and myself in May 1966 is still regarded as one of the finest hours in the history of tennis in Jamaica and the Caribbean.

My son Ryan is also a rising Jamaican and internal tennis star.

I founded the Tennis Academy in Jamaica to train young, promising tennis stars.

JAMAICAN SPORTS TRIVIA 9

I was born December 26, 1989. I attended St. Jago High School in Spanish Town where my first sporting love was cricket. I was a fast bowler and when my principal saw how quickly I ran to the wicket, he urged me to try sprinting. I took his advice and started training in track and field.

2005 CARIFTA Games (Junior)–I earned 2 gold medals in the 100 and 200 meters in Bacelot.

2006 CARIFTA Games (Junior), held in Abymes–I earned 1 gold in 200m and 1 gold in the 4 x 100 relay. That same year 1 gold in 100 and 200 meters and 1 gold in the 4 x 100 relay. At the Beijing World Junior Championships, I earned a bronze in the 100 and gold in the 4 x 100 relays.

2007 CARIFTA Games (Junior), held in Providencials–I earned gold in the 100 meters and the 4 x 100 relay. In that same year I earned a silver in the 100 at Sao Paulo and a bronze in the 4 x 400 relay. I set the fastest time by a Jamaican junior sprinter over 100 meters with a time of 10.11 seconds. The record was set at the 2007 CARIFTA Games in the Turks and Caicos Islands and I led my team to gold in the 4 x 100 meters relay. I was awarded the Austin Sealy Trophy for the most outstanding athlete of the 2007 CARIFTA Games.

2008 CARIFTA Games (Junior), held in Basseterre–I earned gold in the 100 meters and silver in the 4 x 100 relay held in Bydgoszcz. In 2008 when Usain Bolt was asked in an interview whether there was any sprinter that could challenge him, Bolt named me, (his training partner), saying "Watch out for him, he works like a beast. He's there with me step for step in training." The "Beast" nickname has stuck with me ever since.

2011 World Championships in Daegu–I earned gold medals in the 100 meters and in the 4 x 100 relay.

2012 London Olympics–I earned gold in the 4 x 100 relay and silver in the 100 and 200 meters. I am the current world champion over the 100 and a silver medalist in the 100 and 200 meters.

My 100 meters personal best of 9.69 seconds makes me equal to the second fastest man ever with Tyson Gay, and after Usain Bolt. My personal best for the 200 (19.26 seconds) is the second fastest ever after Bolt. I hold the national junior record for the 100 meters, and am the youngest sprinter to have broken the 10 second barrier (at 19 years, 196 days). I am coached by Glen Mills and my training partners are Usain Bolt and Daniel Bailey. I began my 2012 season strong, registering the first sub-10-second time of the season (9.90s) at April's UTech Classic. I registered a 9.84 second run at the Cayman Invitational prior to the Jamaican Olympic trials, where I beat Usain Bolt over 100 metres with a time of 9.75 seconds. I also won the 200 metres with a time of 19.80s ahead of Bolt at 19.83s, but at the 2012 London Olympics Usain Bolt did not relent.

Who Am I?
Music & Entertainment

Tuff Gong–Bob Marley's recording studio in Kingston. Photograph courtesy of the Jamaica Tourist Board

JAMAICAN MUSIC AND ENTERTAINMENT TRIVIA 1

I was born on February 6, 1945 in the village of Nine Mile in Saint Ann, Jamaica. My father was a white Jamaican of mixed descent whose family came from Sussex, England. He married my mother, an Afro-Jamaican when she was only 18 years old. My father died when I was 10 years old from a heart attack at age 70, leaving my mother to raise me.

I had a love for music from an early age; ironically, my musical career lasted for twenty years. During that time my growing style encompassed every aspect in the rise of Jamaican music, from ska to contemporary reggae. My first recording attempts came at the beginning of the Sixties. My first two tunes, cut as a solo artist, meant nothing in commercial terms and it wasn't until 1964, as a founding member of a band that I first hit the Jamaican charts. That growth was well reflected in the maturity of the group's music. Before long we were properly established as one of the hottest groups in Jamaica.

I surrounded myself with brilliant musicians and became a successful songwriter and made a global impact. Some renowned artists have recorded and/or performed some of my songs, (just to name a few); Johnny Nash, Grover Washington Jnr, Chuck Jackson, Eric Clapton, Barbara Streisand also Stevie Wondre's *Master Blaster* was a tribute to me.

1977–I released a top record which established me as an international superstar status. It remained on the British charts for 56 straight weeks, and netted three UK hit singles.

1979–The *Survival* LP was released. A European tour came the following year: the band broke festival records throughout the continent, including a 100,000 capacity show in Milan. At the end of the European tour, we stopped in New York for two scheduled shows in Madison Square Garden, but immediately afterwards I became seriously ill. Cancer was diagnosed.

1980–1981, I was the official guest of the Government of Zimbabwe to play at that country's Independence Ceremony. In June 1981 I was awarded Jamaica's Order of Merit, the nation's third highest honor, in recognition of my outstanding contribution to the country's culture.

I fought the disease for eight months. The battle, however, proved to be too much. I died in a Miami Hospital on May 11, 1981 at the young age of 36; I was survived by my wife, my children and a host of fans around the world.

January 19, 1994–(More fame after my death). I was inducted into the Rock & Roll Hall of Fame. All of my records released by Island Records have sold more than a million copies. *Legend,* one of my best compilations has sold in excess of twelve million copies. It has been on the Billboard pop catalogue charts (albums over four years old), for more than 200 weeks, it held the number one slot for 19 consecutive weeks.

JAMAICAN MUSIC AND ENTERTAINMENT TRIVIA 2

I was born October 6, 1946 in Clarendon, Jamaica.

In my teens, Roy Panton and I recorded for Coxsone Dodd's Studio One.

1963–I Went to Forest Hill, London, to make my fourth recording, an Ernest Ranglin rearrangement of *My Boy Lollipop,* originally released by Barbie Gaye in late 1956.

1964–*My Boy Lollipop;* was released March 1964, my cover was a massive hit, reaching number two both in the UK Singles Chart and in the U.S. Billboard Hot 100. It also topped the chart in Australia. Initially it sold over 600,000 copies in the United Kingdom. *My Boy Lollipop* sold over six million records worldwide and helped to launch Island Record into mainstream popular music.

In the U.S. *My Boy Lollipop* appeared on the Smash Records subsidiary of Mercury Records), I was the first artist to have a hit that was recorded in the bluebeat style. (I was billed as 'The Blue Beat Girl' on the single's label in the U.S.)

I also had minor UK hits with 2 follow-up singles. Later in 1964 peaking at #30 with *Sweet William* and #48 with *Bloodshot Eyes.*

I appeared on the 1964 Beatles TV special Around The Beatles.

On August 6, 2011, being the 49th anniversary of the country's independence, the Governor-General of Jamaica conferred the Order of Distinction in the rank of Commander (CD) upon me for my contribution to the Jamaican music industry.

I lived in Singapore from 1971 to 1973 before returning to the UK which is now my home.

I have an adult daughter, who studied art and also pursued the music industry.

JAMAICAN MUSIC AND ENTERTAINMENT TRIVIA 3

I was born in May Pen, Clarendon, Jamaica in 1945, the youngest of seven children. I grew up singing gospel music in a church choir, and later moved to Kingston at the age of thirteen.

In Kingston, I met Henry and Jerry and later formed a harmonious singing group that was destined to succeed.

1963–Our group won the first-ever Jamaican Independence Festival Song Competition with our original song *Bam Bam*.

1969–My group and I won the Jamaican Independence Festival Song Competition for the 2nd time; *Sweet and Dandy*.

1971–Our song; *Monkey Man* became our first international hit.

1972–We won the Jamaican Independence Festival Song Competition for the third time, with our popular festival song; *Pomp's and Pride*.

1972–Our group was also featured twice in the soundtrack to *The Harder They Come,* the 1972 film starring Jimmy Cliff.

I turned a negative into a positive when I wrote the hit song; *54-46 That's My Number.*

We now have an international presence in the music industry.

I was often compared to Otis Redding.

JAMAICAN MUSIC AND ENTERTAINMENT TRIVIA 4

I was born October 17, 1968, in, Trench Town Jamaica, the son of a famed reggae musician.

1979–My siblings and I did a recording with our father, *Children Playing in the Streets.* Our group was called; The Melody Makers.

In 1991, the Melody Makers and I contributed the song *Give A Little Love* to the Disney album, For Our Children. The album is a collection of kid-friendly songs by popular artists (e.g. Paul McCartney, Bruce Springsteen and Elton John), with proceeds given to the Pediatric AIDS Foundation.

The Melody Makers and I made a guest appearance on the popular kids television show Sesame Street in the 1991-92 seasons, and sang a Sesame Street version of *Small People* from their 1991 album *Jahmekya*.

I made guest appearances on an episode of the sitcom *Family Matters* in 1995, and on the television series *Charmed* in season 6 (episode 14, *The Legend of Sleepy Halliwell*), performing *Rainbow in the Sky.*

On July 2, 2006, my second solo album, *Love Is My Religion,* was released on my independent record company Tuff Gong Worldwide. This album won a Grammy for best Reggae album, which was my 4th Grammy win.

On May 5, 2009, my third solo children's album *Family Time,* was released on my independent record company Tuff Gong Worldwide. *Family Time* features Family and Friends, this album won a Grammy for "Best Musical Album for Children".

Some of my most popular singles include *True To Myself, Drive, People Get Ready,* and my US Top 40 and US Top 20 hit *Tomorrow People.*

In April 2011, I released my fourth album, entitled *Wild and Free* also my first comic book.

I founded Unlimited Resources Giving Enlightenment (URGE), which works to help children (especially in Jamaica and Ethiopia).

In 2007, I signed on as an official supporter of Little Kids Rock, a nonprofit organization that provides free musical instruments and free lessons to children in public schools throughout the United States. I have visited with children in the program and I sit on the organization's board of directors as an honorary member. I am married, with six children.

JAMAICAN MUSIC AND ENTERTAINMENT TRIVIA 5

I was born March 28, 1926; I was the only child of Edgar and Gladys, until the birth of my sister twenty years later.

I was an avid reader of Popular Mechanics magazine, which led me to build my own radio, allowing me to listen to music from Cuba and the United States.

I taught myself how to read music and play the trumpet, my professional work as a musician came with Eric Deans' orchestra.

I later formed my own band which became renowned for recreating the sound of a 14-piece orchestra with only seven musicians and that led to Jamaican Big Band, featuring some of Jamaica's top musicians. For over 14 years I served as the president of the Jamaican Federation of Musicians.

1979–I founded the Tastee Talent Contest (later known as the Tastee Talent Trail), which played a major part in launching the careers of artists including Yellowman, Beenie Man, Mr. Vegas, T.O.K., Papa San, Mad Cobra & Brian and Tony Gold.

1991–My wife and I founded the Ocho Rios Jazz Festival.

2004–I was awarded the Order of Distinction, Commander Class by the Jamaican government for my contribution to Jamaican music.

2008–I was honored by the Miramar City Commission at a ceremony to mark the opening of the Miramar Cultural Arts Center in Florida in my contribution to music in Jamaica and abroad.

2009–I suffered a stroke while in London in August, and remained in hospital until my death on the 10th of October, at the age of 83.

JAMAICAN MUSIC AND ENTERTAINMENT TRIVIA 6

I was born April 1, 1948 in St. James, Jamaica. I began writing songs while still at primary school.

1962–My father took me to Kingston to attend Technical school where I shared a rented room with my cousin.

At 14 I had a big hit; *Hurricane Hattie.*

1960s–My career took off, my international debut album was *Hard Road to Travel,* which received excellent reviews and included *Waterfall* (composed by Nirvana's Alex Spyropoulos and Patrick Campbell-Lyons), which became a hit in Brazil and won the International Song Festival.

1964–I was chosen as one of the Jamaican representatives at the World's Fair and soon signed to Island Records and moved to the UK. I am best known among mainstream audiences for songs such as *Sitting in Limbo, You Can Get It If You Really Want,* and *Many Rivers to Cross* from the soundtrack to *The Harder They Come,* which helped popularize reggae across the world.

2010–I was one of five performers inducted into the Rock and Roll Hall of Fame.

1972–I played the lead role in a classic reggae film, which remains the most significant film to have come out of Jamaica since its independence.

1990–One of my song's; *You Can Get It If You Really Want* was used as a campaign anthem by the Sandinista National Liberation Front in the 1990 election in Nicaragua.

1995–I released the single *Hakuna Matata,* a collaboration with Lebo M, a song from the soundtrack of the film *The Lion King.*

2007–*You Can Get It If You Really Want,* was also adopted by the British Conservative Party during their annual conference in October 2007.

I appeared on the Jazz World Stage at the Glastonbury Festival in 2008 and again at Glastonbury in 2011.

As a Jamaican musician, singer and actor, currently I am the only living musician to hold the Order of Merit, the highest honor that can be granted by the Jamaican government for achievement in the arts and sciences.

JAMAICAN MUSIC AND ENTERTAINMENT TRIVIA 7

I was born on 1 February 1957 at Jubilee Hospital in Kingston, Jamaica; my father was a scriptwriter, actor, and journalist. I grew up in a large tenement yard between North Street and King Street in Kingston with my parents, three elder brothers and a sister. My mother died in the 1960s.

I attended Central Branch Primary School and later St. Stephens College. I began my singing career at the age of nine and cited Nat King Cole as one of my greatest early influences.

Relatives and neighbors would often throw me pennies to hear me sing in their yard. My first professional appearance came at the age of eleven.

My first recording was an original song called *Lips of Wine* for producer Derrick Harriott, but when this was not released, I recorded for Clement "Coxsone," Dodd's Studio One label, my first session yielded the single *No Man is an Island,* recorded when I was twelve and released in late 1969.

Bob Marley dubbed me "The Crown Prince of Reggae."

My 1994 album *Light My Fire* was nominated for a Grammy Award

I died on July 1, 1999 leaving my wife and thirteen children. At my funeral both the Prime Minister of Jamaica and the Leader of the Opposition spoke.

Two of my top hits; *Money in my Pocket* and *Westbound Train.*

JAMAICAN MUSIC AND ENTERTAINMENT TRIVIA 8

I was born in the year 1952 in Gordon Town, St. Andrew Jamaica. My family was poor and although no one went hungry, we could not afford a radio in the house. As a child, singing came as naturally to me as breathing and I was always 'singled-out' for solo spots with church choirs. At 13 years old I became a member of a dance group which toured Jamaica and other islands in the Caribbean.

Some of my earliest influences were; Aretha Franklin, Otis Redding, Curtis Mayfield, Dionne Warwick, Bob Marley, Marcia Griffiths, The Staple Singers and The Soulettes.

1967–I was a founding member of the Gaylettes Dance Trio.

I had written some of the tracks recorded by Bunny Wailer.

1974–I joined Marcia Griffiths and Rita Marley to form the 'I-Threes,' Back-Ground vocalists for Bob Marley.

1985–I became the first female singer nominated for a GRAMMY in the category of reggae music when my *Working Wonders* LP was nominated. I was the first female reggae artist to appear on Late Night with David Letterman, when I made my debut that same year. My *Black Woman* LP is considered by many critics to be the greatest reggae LP done by a female artist. 'It was the first reggae LP recorded by a woman acting as her own producer.'

My commitment to meaningful lyrics made me a renowned advocate of important issues concerning women, spiritual inspiration and African liberation. *Love is Overdue* included on the *Shanachie* LP made me the first female reggae singer to score a major American pop hit.

I was a devoted Rastafarian for twenty-two years, desiring to please God all the way; I suddenly became overshadowed with a feeling of emptiness and total dissatisfaction. In 1995 hunger for the whole truth arose and I knew instantly this marked the end of my search. I now know that "Jesus is the Way, the truth and the life."

I have broadened my repertoire with a series of gospel songs and I'm now busily spreading the Gospel of Jesus Christ. After recording my *Love* CD I released my second gospel album entitled *Something Old, Something New.*

I now have an international ministry and I go wherever I am called to sing.

I am a devoted mother to my five children.

JAMAICAN MUSIC AND ENTERTAINMENT TRIVIA 9

I was born June 27, 1935, in Christiana, Manchester, Jamaica. Years later I became a musician, record producer, and entrepreneur.

As a young child I learned to play the piano at a convent school in Mandeville, but I put music on hold when I became a member of the Jamaican national football team.

I taught myself to play bass on a homemade instrument, and I and my friend Carl formed a band that was named after the college football team that we played for.

I was the first one to have introduced the electric bass guitar to Jamaica, which quickly gained popularity throughout the country and soon became the standard.

I also worked as a producer, producing many of the ska singles by The Maytals. I became the head of distribution in Jamaica for Atlantic Records.

I purchased the West Indies Records Limited (WIRL) recording studios from Edward Seaga after fire had destroyed the pressing plant on the same site, and renamed it Dynamic Sounds.

Dynamic Sounds became one of Jamaica's leading record distributors attracting both local and international recording artists, including Paul Simon and The Rolling Stones, who recorded their famous song *Angie*. My productions included Boris Gardiner's *Reggae Happening*, Hopeton Lewis's *Grooving Out on Life*, and The Slickers' *Johnny Too Bad*.

I made the US charts in mid 60s.

In 1990, I inaugurated what became an annual event; the Jamaica Carnival, held on Constant Spring Road. Some of my hits were; *Tiny Winey, Soca Bogle, Soca Butterfly* and *Soca Tatie*.

I missed the Jamaica Carnival in 2007, due to my battle with cancer. A concert was held in my honor on June 30, 2007, to celebrate my 50 years in the music industry, with artists performing including fellow cancer-survivors Myrna Hague and Pluto Shervington. Proceeds went to the Jamaica Cancer Society.

In October 2008, after receiving treatment for several weeks in Florida, I returned to Jamaica to spend my final days. In a ceremony at the University Hospital of the West Indies on October 26, 2008, I was awarded the Order of Jamaica (OJ).

I died on November 4, 2008, aged 73. In a statement on the day of my death, the Prime Minister of Jamaica, Bruce Golding, said "Jamaica, and indeed the world, has lost another great music pioneer with the passing this morning of -------, one of the greatest band leaders ever to grace the entertainment stages of the world."

Who Am I?

Theatre & Art

JAMAICAN THEATER AND ART TRIVIA 1

I was born February 14, 1931.

1962–After having a successful Theatrical career in England I was invited to return to Jamaica for a performance in Nuggets for the Needy, where I was afforded the opportunity to work with Sammy Davis Jr. for the second time. My visit home was extended from two weeks to three months to allow me the opportunity to perform in the Independence Revival of the LTM's Carib Gold. On my return to England, I ventured into the Off West End Production of *Do Something Addy Man* and realized new adventures in my professional career in Britain and Europe.

1962 - 1973–I appeared and starred in several television, radio, stage and cabaret productions for the BBC, ITV, Grenada and London Week-end Television, BBC Home, Third Light and Caribbean Radio Services which featured productions such as *Crown Court, Love thy Neighbour* and *Blood Knot*. During my theatrical career, I toured Britain and Europe with several productions for the Oxford Playhouse and other professional theatrical groups. My film career in England included *High Wind in Jamaica, Crossplot, Bush Babies* and *Love Thy Neighbour*. While in England, I made over 200 appearances on radio and over 50 on television.

1974–I returned to Jamaica and rejoined the JBC as the head of the Department of Theatre and also was the producer and director of the popular radio serial *Fortunes of Floralee*. I was also the presenter of the Musical Show, *Sunday Souvenirs*. During this time I also appeared in several productions including *Macbeth, Two's a Crowd, Sex, Brashanio, Mother Courage, The Mouse Trap, Old Story Time* and *Johnny Reggae*. During this time I also wrote, directed and produced plays which included *The Last of the Red Hot Lovers, Jesus Christ dem kill Son Son, Curly Locks and The Seven DJ's* and *Santa Fari*. I also produced and directed the following for radio: *Ritual: For a new Liberation Covenant* and *The Rope and the Cross*.

1977–I was awarded Actor of the Year for several productions, which I also produced and directed.

1978–I was awarded a Silver Musgrave Medal by the Institute of Jamaica

1989–My book was published, *When me was a boy* in which I give readers insight into some aspects of Jamaican social life and customs. This book was published by the Institute of Jamaica in 1989.

1980–I was awarded the Institute Centenary Medal and a national honor–the Order of Distinction.

I was; Actor, Comedian, Director, Writer and Radio and Television Broadcaster and I died January 1, 2007.

JAMAICAN THEATER AND ART TRIVIA 2

I was born on February 10, 1911 (My career as an Artist began in the 1930's).

1964 and 1968; I held exhibitions in Washington D.C.

1966–I was awarded a Gold Medal from Emperor Haile Selassie during his visit to Jamaica.

1969–I was awarded the Silver Musgrave Medal from the Institute of Jamaica.

1969 and 1982–I held exhibitions in New York.

1972–I held exhibitions in Los Angeles.

1977–I was awarded the Order of Distinction by the Government of Jamaica.

1981–My painting, *Shining Spring* was chosen as a wedding gift to Prince Charles and Lady Diana Spencer from the Government and people of Jamaica. *Shining Spring* was selected by the Institute of Jamaica, along with the Office of the Prime Minister because it was felt to be representative of true Jamaican art.

1985–I was awarded the 'Norman Manley Award for Excellence' in the Fine Arts.

1986–I was awarded the Gold Musgrave Medal from the Institute of Jamaica.

I was married twice. I died on February 24, 1989.

JAMAICAN THEATER AND ART TRIVIA 3

I was born in 1900 to a Jamaican mother and an English father. I played a major pioneering role in the history of 20th century Jamaican art.

In 1921, I married my cousin and moved to Jamaica with him in 1922. We had two children, one a future prime minister and the other a sociologist and minister of government. My husband entered politics, and founded the People's National Party in 1938. Every phase of my life is expressed through Art so I designed The Rising Sun logo for the People's National Party. The beginning of Jamaica's new government–and the fall of colonialism–was reflected in my work.

The 1950s and 1960s were quiet times for me as an artist. My husband became more involved with politics and with my new responsibilities it left little time for art. In 1965, I created a statue of Paul Bogle to commemorate his partaking in Jamaica's Morant Bay Rebellion. The statue was highly controversial because it was inherently the very first Jamaican public statue that depicted a black man. My husband became ill and was laid to rest in 1969.

Throughout my career I passed through a series of phases, each representing stages in the development of my life and that of Jamaica:

1969-1974–'A Period of Mourning.' This was the period of illness and death of my beloved husband. So I turned to my talent and created; *Angel, the Grief of Mary, Journey* among others.

1974–I stopped carving in wood with *Journey* and all my subsequent works were carved in clay and cast.

1977–I received the Honorary Degree of Doctor of Letters from the University of West Indies, Kingston.

1980–At the National Gallery Retrospective Exhibition I was awarded; 'The Order of Merit'

1987–I died on February 2, .

My work is displayed in private collections, galleries and public buildings worldwide.

JAMAICAN THEATER AND ART TRIVIA 4

I was born on September 7, 1919. I received my education from Ebenezer and Calabar Elementary Schools, St. Simon's College, Excelsior College, Friends College (Highgate).

I was described as Jamaica's leading comedian, as the "only poet who has really hit the truth about my society through its own language", and as an important contributor to my country of "valid social documents reflecting the way Jamaicans think and feel and live." Through my poems in Jamaican patois, I raised the dialect of the Jamaican folk to an art level which is acceptable to and appreciated by all in Jamaica.

In my poems I was able to capture all the spontaneity of the expression of Jamaicans' joys and sorrows, their ready, poignant and even wicked wit, their religion and their philosophy of life. My first dialect poem was written when I was only fourteen years old. A British Council Scholarship took me to the Royal Academy of Dramatic Art where I studied. After graduation I worked with repertory companies in Coventry, Huddersfield and Amersham as well as in intimate revues all over England.

I lectured extensively in the United States and the United Kingdom on Jamaican folklore and music and represented Jamaica all over the world. I married Eric Winston (who died in 2002). I have one stepson and several adopted children. I enjoyed Theatre, Movies and Auction sales.

1972–I received the Norman Manley Foundation award for Excellence.

1974–I was awarded the Institute of Jamaica's Musgrave Silver and Gold Medals for distinguished eminence in the field of Arts and Culture.

1988–My composition *You're going home now,* won a nomination from the Academy of Canadian Cinema ad Television, for the best original song in the movie *Milk and Honey.*

1998–I received the Honorary Degree of Doctor of Letters from York University, Toronto, Canada.

2001–The Jamaica Government also appointed me Cultural Ambassador at Large for Jamaica, on August 6, 2001. I was appointed as a Member of the Order of Merit for my distinguished contribution to the development of the Arts and Culture.

Having lived in Toronto, Canada for over ten years I developed a large Canadian following.

I died on July 27, 2006 at 87 years old...

JAMAICAN THEATER AND ART TRIVIA 5

I was born November 4, 1948 in Harmony Hall, St. Mary. My involvement in drama began when I was only six years old.

I attended the Salvation Army School in my district then Rose Bank Primary and then I attended high school in Highgate, after which I went to the Dinthill Technical High School. There was no scope for the advancement for my love for drama and creativity at Dinthill. After school I worked as a storekeeper at the Orange River Agricultural Station and later moved to Kingston on the advice of my friends. I landed a clerical job at the National Water Commission and then took a job proofreading at the Gleaner Company, which only lasted for one day. Unfilled, so I knew I had to pursue my dream.

1971-1973, I attended The Jamaica Theatre School; my life tells the story of a poor boy that made good.

During my three years at the Jamaica Theatre School, I participated in various productions. My first play was *A Raisin in the Sun.*

I have appeared in no less than 13 pantomimes playing major roles, some of my pantomime appearances include, *Queenie's Daughter, Hail Columbus, Dickance for Fippance, Pirate Princess, Ginneral B* and *Music Boy.*

I have also appeared in overseas productions such as *The Fight Against Slavery,* the British Broadcasting Corporation's television series aired it in 1974. There were other BBC productions such as *My Father Son-Son Johnson, Chef* and *Brothers and Sisters.*

I appeared as Son-Son in *Royal Palm Estate* produced by Lennie Little-White.

I have my own television series, which has established me locally and internationally.

I am an avid reader of politics, social affairs and religion.

I am the proud father of 6 children and some adorable grand children.

My words of wisdom; "Be humble, humility can take you anywhere."

JAMAICAN THEATER AND ART TRIVIA 6

I was born on June 14 and grew up as an only child, I believe I was born acting, because it comes naturally.

My first job was a typist with Sir Philip Sherlock and then I worked with University College of the West Indies (UCWI). After a while I went to work with Barry Reckord, a playwright and he introduced me to the world of Broadcasting.

I spent six years at the Royal Academy of Dramatic Arts, (RADA), in England.

I appeared in several RADA productions including the pantomime *Cinderella.* I also played in *Unknown Woman of Arras, Days of the Lion,* and *Antony and Cleopatra* in which I was the lead female actor. I was also featured in television drama series on the BBC and Independent Television networks such as Z Cars, Odd Man, Public Eye, Hugh and I, Desperate People and Harper's West.

1962–April was my first appearance in professional theatre, *Busha Blue Beard,* a Lloyd Reckord production.

1966–I returned to Jamaica Broadcasting Corporation (JBC), after my training at RADA.

1968 - 1970–I left for Australia two years later, while there I appeared in the production of the Shakespearean play *Merchant of Venice.* I returned to Jamaica and JBC.

1972–I spearheaded the development of Radio Two JBC FM Stereo Service and started and ran the JBC TV Drama Work Shop, which produced among other programs; *Stronger, A Scent of Jasmine, and Lets Say Grace*–a screenplay which I wrote and produced.

1976–May, I was appointed to the post of Director of Radio Broadcasting for the JBC.

1980 - 1981–I appeared in the film *Children of Babylon* and *Milk and Honey.*

1995–*What My Mother Told Me* and *Soul Survivor.*

2001–I was awarded "My Life in the Theatre" medal by the Mexican Theatre Centre of the International Theatre Institute for outstanding theatre personalities of Latin America and the Caribbean, along with many other awards.

I have authored a book titled, *The Re-Entry into Sound,* along with Alma Mock Yen, This is a standard text used to train broadcasters all over the Caribbean. I am the proud mother of four children.

JAMAICAN THEATER AND ART TRIVIA 7

I was born on February 3, 1933. I was a Jamaican scholar, graduated from Cornwall College in Montego Bay and then continued my studies at the University of the West Indies where I obtained an honors degree in history.

I was a recipient of a Rhodes Scholarship to Oriel College in Oxford where I received a postgraduate degree in Politics, and returned to Jamaica in the early 1960s to take up a position at the University of the West Indies.

1962–I founded the National Dance Theatre Company of Jamaica, an ensemble which under my direction did much to incorporate traditional Jamaican Music and dance into a formal balletic repertoire.

I was the Artistic Director for the University Singers of the University of the West Indies, Mona campus in Jamaica.

1968–I took over the direction of the School for Continuing Studies at the University and then of the Extra-Mural Department.

1969–I published the collection of essays Mirror, Mirror.

1975–I was awarded the Order of Merit for my cultural and scholarly achievements.

1996–I became Vice-Chancellor of the University of the West Indies and held that office until 2004.

I established myself as a serious public historian and social critic.

2008–I was awarded the Caribbean region's highest honor, the Order of the Caribbean Community (OCC) for my years of dedicated service as a regional ambassador. This award cemented me as the quintessential Caribbean citizen and international cultural icon.

On January 27, 2010, I was admitted to the intensive care unit of the George Washington University hospital, Washington DC, after suffering a heart attack at my hotel room.

On Tuesday, February 2, 2010, I was pronounced dead at around 8:00 pm EST.

It is believed that I have left an indelible mark on the history of Jamaica and the entire Caribbean.

JAMAICAN THEATER AND ART TRIVIA 8

I was born in Kingston on March 24, 1940 and was raised in Bellas Gate, an isolated hillside community in rural St Catherine. I was the youngest child of a very large family, my father; a farmer was married twice and had 23 children.

Although my childhood was impoverished, a desire to succeed was instilled by my parents and teachers.

During my high school years I discovered that I had a love for the theatre and became actively involved in the Secondary Schools Drama Festival, as well as the annual pantomime staged by the Little Theatre Movement. After graduation, I began writing radio plays for the newly established Jamaica Broadcasting Corporation (JBC).

1960 - 1965–I went to London on a scholarship to attend the Rose Bruford Training College of Speech and Drama. Back in Jamaica I formed a dramatic arts group, Theatre 77, with Yvonne Jones-Brewster and other colleagues, and later opened the Barn Theatre in a converted garage.

1969–I concentrated on writing my first stage play, *The Gadget*–which explored the tensions that developed between an illiterate countrywoman and her urbanized, educated son.

1970 - 1971–I collaborated with Perry Henzell on *The Harder They Come,* the acclaimed cinematic masterpiece about a country boy forced into a life of crime and violence by the dehumanization of the city. With Jimmy Cliff in the lead role and a reggae soundtrack featuring Desmond Dekker and Toots and the Maytals, *The Harder They Come* made a tremendous impact overseas.

1972–I achieved great success at home with *Smile Orange* (1971), a biting satire written largely in dialect that exposed Caribbean tourism as a stilted series of duplicitous exchanges, its machinations mired in exploitative greed, envy, and stereotypical assumptions about race. In most of my work humor is used to explore deeply troubling subjects.

In addition to *Smile Orange,* I have written other screenplays/films, such as; *Comic Strip, Sleeper, School's Out* and *Old Story Time, Two Can Play* and *Milk and Honey.*

I wrote the screenplay *One Love* in 2003, which starred Bob Marley's son Ky-mani as a rasta musician who has a problematic love affair with a Christian. I have received many civic awards during my life, but the most notable being; Commander of the Order of Distinction by the Jamaican government. Up to the time of my death on September 15, 2009, I had been working on several projects. I am survived by my wife, Camille, and children Traci, Trevor Jr. and Jonathan.

JAMAICAN THEATER AND ART TRIVIA 9

I was born in Colon Panama on October 26, 1912. I came to Jamaica at the age of six. I was educated at Tutorial College, Calabar High School and Kingston Technical High School.

I was a dramatist and comedian, and first started my acting career as a child reciting poetry at church, Lodge Hall and schoolrooms.

As a comedian and actor I teamed with Miss Lou (Louise Bennett) so we became leaders in Jamaican comedy. I went on to appear in pantomines, films and on television. My first pantomime was *Bluebeard and Brer Anancy* in 1942, and would appear in almost every pantomime thereafter in the 50s, 60s and 70s..

I hosted my own television show in Jamaica in the 60s and I also appeared in movies like, *A High Wind in Jamaica, Oh Dad Poor Dad, White Souls, Jamaica No Problem, Tropical Isles, Zacc Experience* and *The Marijuana Affair.*

I had many outstanding achievements in the field of entertainment and drama. After decades of serving my country and bringing laughter to Jamaicans across the globe, I went to rest on August 11, 1980.

JAMAICAN THEATER AND ART TRIVIA 10

I was born in Lucea, Jamaica in the parish of Hanover, on January 9, 1931. I loved art at a young age and felt called to follow my passion despite my parents' desire for me to become a lawyer.

I was educated at Kingston College where I started out as an athlete, but eventually decided to follow my heart to pursue art overseas. I traveled to England to study at the London School of Printing and Graphic Art and from there I was accepted to the Royal College of Art. My diverse art schooling took me to art academies in Amsterdam, Madrid, Rome, and Paris where I studied African, Asian, European and American artwork. My exposure to the world was partnered with my love for the Caribbean, to create paintings that stand out among other island artwork.

In 1961, I returned to Jamaica and was hired as an art appreciation professor at the University of The West Indies. I became the first director of studies for the Jamaica School of Art in 1962. I grew passionate towards nurtured aspiring young artists, but I never let go of my dream of becoming a professional artist. In the late 1960s I began to gain widespread popularity as a painter. Through my artwork, I detail the history, culture and story of the black race. I have painted portraits of black historical figures such as Fredrick Douglass, Harriet Tubman, W.E.B. Du Bois, Malcolm X, Rosa Parks, and Martin Luther King, Jr. Yet, I am most well known for painting the female form. Through my abundant works that feature the female form, I use it as a forum to express my high respect and regard for women. I want to capture the heart of Jamaica and its people. I paint figures dressed in traditional Jamaican clothing and fills the backdrops of my paintings with bright tones that encapsulate the vibrant atmosphere of the Caribbean.

My paintings come to life through a variety of mediums including oils, pencil, crayon, pen and watercolor. I also use the careful layering of color to create the beautiful variety of skin tones in my work. I blend European style and techniques with Caribbean landscapes and figures to form my original style.

I have always focused on the importance of the development of the art community in Jamaica and has advocated for building more art institutions on the islands. In 1964, I founded the Contemporary Jamaican Artists Association, which promoted art as a social vehicle for change. I was one of three artists active in the association; my partners were Jamaican Painters Eugene Hyde and Karl Parboosingh. Today, I am the only surviving founder of the association and still operates the Contemporary Art Center, which I established in the early 1980s.

I created a Gallery named after me in 1974, the Jamaica Art Foundation in 1985, the Orange Park Trust in 1991 and the Pan-Africanists Committee in 1998. I have written several books and I continue to make history as I paint and teach from my Orange Park Studios gallery in St. Thomas.

Who Am I?
Media

Barbara Ellington–well known Jamaican journalist

JAMAICAN MEDIA TRIVIA 1

I started out in journalism as a feature writer for the Daily News. I loved experimenting with style. I read a lot of profiles in Vanity Fair Esquire. *The 7 Laws of Success* by Herbert Armstrong, has left a big influence on my early life and I thought why not use journalism to reach a wide audience and thereby show everyone how to overcome difficulties. Olivia 'Babsy' Grange introduced me to Gloria Lanaman who then sent me to the late Don Bucknor at the then Jamaica Broadcasting Corporation (JBC). My first guest was Carlton Alexander of Grace Kennedy and I have not looked back since that day.

In 1981, I was awarded for distinguished religious writing. I won a total of four national journalism awards, both in Print and in Television, the first won at age 18 for in-depth profiles done on writer John Maxwell, intellectual Rex Nettleford and South African author Peter Abrahams. I have been press secretary for 12 ministers of government, on both sides of the political divide.

I am seriously into time management. I can't stand to waste time, my ability to get so much done in one day is no doubt a major contributor to my achievements.

Some of the best moments of my career, were due not to mere skill but to a "reputation for fairness." The interview with Lee Malvo's Mother, Una James propelled me to the front page of the Washington Post, to an interview with FOX network and which led to deals with several other international media houses, including NBC.

I have the record of the longest-running non-seasonal programme on Jamaican television, the 25th anniversary of my show was celebrated on Wednesday, February 22, 2012. I am also the only Jamaican journalist with shows on radio, television and a column in print. I have been in print from 1975 and television since 1976 (JIS).

My work in journalism has some overarching objectives: to inspire and motivate (Profile); to enlighten and intellectually stimulate (Gleaner columns) and to foster tolerance and diversity (Religious Hardtalk). On Heroes Day 2009 I received the Order of Distinction in the rank of Commander (CD) for contribution to the field of journalism. It was the ultimate honour.

I have learned from some of the best in the business like Mike Wallace, Diane Sawyer, Tim Russert and Peter Jennings. And I compare the success and longevity of *Profile* only with similar series on the international scene. My goal is to promote success stories of persons who have risen above extreme adversity and emerged victorious when the odds were against them.

My daughter Kelly is an attorney and I am proud of her. I am married to Margaret.

JAMAICAN MEDIA TRIVIA 2

I grew up in Rollington Town, East Kingston. My father was a railway station master and my mother a housewife. In the 1960s I came to public attention as an accomplished model, radio broadcaster with the Jamaica Broadcasting Corporation (JBC) and businesswoman.

On June 10, 1972, I married the man who was believed to be Jamaica's most charismatic leader. His mother hosted a quiet ceremony in her back gardens.

Shortly after the marriage I began championing gender issues, recalling that I had grown up with a strong mother who believed in the economic independence of women so that men could not take advantage of them. I wanted to help women achieve economic independence that was one of the driving motives behind my support for the controversial 'Crash Program' of the 1970s which was "a way of giving quick employment to large numbers of poor women".

I also pushed for many of the social legislation benefiting women in particular, such as equal pay for women, which came during 1970s, and helped to position Jamaica in the international thrust to ameliorate the conditions of women. I was elected president of the PNP Women's Movement, I was a part of a process that led the changes in legislation that discriminated against women and children. In addition, I have had the opportunity to meet some notable world leaders, just to name a few; Jimmy Carter, Pierre Trudeau, Fidel Castro. I became the sixth Director of the Bureau of Women's Affairs (BWA).

After eighteen years the marriage ended and I was able to reinvent myself, "picking myself up, getting on with my life." On Monday March 2, 1992 at 6:00 a.m. I assisted Anthony "Tony" Abrahams to bring to life the Breakfast Club on KLAS FM. The program created an explosion on the airwaves. Tony and I built it together. Building it meant setting up a database of experts from all over the world that we call on for almost any issue. After investing 13 years in the Breakfast Club it was hard to walk away but I was called to write my memoirs.

In an interview with Desmond Allen many years ago I was asked if I would marry again. I never say never, I have been in a committed relationship for at least 20 years (at the time of the interview). "I don't need money, what I need is somebody who loves me enough to allow me to be me in a non-judgmental way." Well, a 32 year love affair, culminated in marriage on Saturday January 21, 2012, I married my partner and best friend.

I have two biological children.

JAMAICAN MEDIA TRIVIA 3

Vice Mayor, News Director at WAVS 1170, Adjunct Professor at Florida Memorial University, Miami Gardens and Committed Family man. Sometimes I find it difficult balancing my life but I love every aspect of it and it's about time management.

I am a proud thirteen-year resident of the City of Miramar and an eighteen-year resident of Broward County. Filling the role of Vice Mayor of Miramar means a lot and because of my access to the media, I am often referred to as; 'the voice for the people.'

I was elected to the City of Miramar Commission in March of 2003. I have served on a number of advisory boards at the Broward County level and am the recipient of numerous awards from various organizations for service to the community for the last 24 years.

I am also the News Director at WAVS 1170 AM Radio in Fort Lauderdale. If you remember the days when JBC existed and there were only two radio stations, there will be no doubt as to who I am. I was one of Jamaica's most notable disc jocks and television hosts. I am also the brother of two noted radio personalities. I left Jamaica in the early 80's after working with RJR and JBC for over 12 years.

I am also involved in activities in the youth department of Christway Baptist Church where I serve as an usher.

I hold a Master's of Science degree from Florida International University and a Bachelor's degree from The New York Institute of Technology (Magna Cum Laude).

In addition to making the time to indulge in hobbies like reading and photography, I also make time to take dictates from my daughter Hannah. I am an avid supporter of leisure biking and I see it as a way to get exercise, stay in shape and spend quality time with my family. I am married to Andrea, and we are proud parents to our eight year old daughter, Hannah. My mother, Beryl and nephew, Franklin, also live in Miramar. I am proud to live in a city like Miramar with good schools, jobs, and a great quality of life.

JAMAICAN MEDIA TRIVIA 4

I was born in Halifax, Manchester on May 6, 1944 and the eldest of three children. I grew up around music, so at an early age I had a deep appreciation for music. I migrated to Bronx, New York in 1962.

I hosted a radio show in New York for several years and relocated to South Florida in 1978. I had to convince radio officials at WLRN, FM 91.3, of my music's popularity so they would put my program, *Sounds of the Caribbean* on the air. But with hard work and a passion for music, I was able to grow the Miami-based show from one to seven nights a week.

I acquired the name; 'The Godfather of Reggae' and I have to thank Bob Marley for encouraging me to host my own radio show. Bob was a frequent visitor on *Sounds of the Caribbean.*

I have been told that I have a trademark laugh, which would often single me out even when I try to go unnoticed.

During my program I'd feature; reggae, calypso, Haitian kompa and Caribbean oldies. I had an international audience and I had an open door policy where I'd interview Stars in the music industry, yet I'd welcome the ordinary man in the studio and allow him to just come in and experience the thrill of the beat.

I have coached younger disc jockeys and artists to perform live on my show. In addition, a Foundation was named after me to help the needy kids of Jamaica. I served this cause up to the time I was diagnosed with colon and lung cancer.

Despite the illness I received proclamations from Miami-Dade County, the State of Florida and the government of Jamaica for my contributions to music and for promoting Caribbean culture.

On October 10, 2004, I said my final farewell; it was a lot different from the one I'd say at the end of every show; "Mi gaan a mi yard, yah."

I was survived by my four children, my sister, brother and a host of close friends and relatives.

Who Am I?

Education & Literary Works

Shine Bright   Leneen Faith

A Guide From Domestic Violence   NINA HART

COME UP DEEPER   DR. CISLIN WILLIAMS

DEADLY NEGLIGENCE   DIANA WRIGHT

Deadly Negligence

Diana

NINA HART
A DEDICATION TO SINGLE MOTHERS

CROSSES TO BEAR LOVE TO SHARE

CROSSES
TO BEAR LOVE TO SHARE

JAMAICAN EDUCATION/LITERARY TRIVIA 1

I was born in St. James on July 2, 1925, I became an orphan by the time I was six, due to the death of my father and mother. I have had a long and distinguished career in education, which started at the age of 16½ when I became a student teacher.

1970–I was awarded The Silver Musgrave Medal of the Institute of Jamaica for outstanding contribution to Public Library Work in Jamaica.

1973–I spearheaded the National Literacy Program and under my leadership it was a huge success, the name changed to Jamaica Movement for the Advancement of Literacy (JAMAL).

1973–I was named; Honorary Vice President by the Library Association of Great Britain.

1975–I was awarded Commander of The Order of Distinction (CD) by the Government of Jamaica for Public Service in the field of Librarianship and Literacy.

1976–I formally became Director of the JAMAL Foundation and remained in that position until 1981.

Up to 1979, 200,000 adult readers graduated from JAMAL.

1979–I received The Carl Milan Lecture Award by the American Library Association. Special International Award to lecture in 12 university library schools in the United States and Canada.

1979–Honorary Degree of Doctor of Laws by the Dalhousie University, Nova Scotia, Canada, for outstanding pioneering work in Libraries and Literacy.

1981-1982–I served as General Manager for the Jamaica Broadcasting Corporation.

1982–I was appointed to address the unemployment problems among young people; the Human Employment and Resource Training (HEART) agency was launched.

1985–I received Woman of Distinction Award (Bureau of Women's Affairs).

1990–I was awarded Honorary Degree of Laws LL.D by the University of the West Indies, Mona for outstanding pioneering work in Library and Literacy

1991–I retired from active employment

I am the mother of two children; Dr. Ann Bridgewater and Anthony Robinson.

I went to rest on May 12, 2013.

JAMAICAN EDUCATION/LITERARY TRIVIA 2

I was born in 1937 and I was, educated at Munro College, the University of the West Indies and St. Edmund Hall, Oxford has built a solid reputation as a literary critic and essayist as well as one of Jamaica's leading poets.

1960's–My work continued to appear widely in Caribbean, Commonwealth and British publications. By late 60's I had built a solid reputation as a literary critic and essayist as well as one of Jamaica's leading poets.

1963–I won Essay Competition with a notable piece entitled, *Feeling, Affection, Respect,* and had essays and poems broadcast by the BBC before returning to Jamaica

1964–I was awarded first prize On Reading Louise Bennett *Seriously,* in the Jamaica Festival Literary Competition.

1968–My essay, *Power and Us* again claimed the first prize in the Jamaica Festival Literary Competition

Long Lives Literary...

JAMAICAN EDUCATION/LITERARY TRIVIA 3

I was born in 1945 to a schoolteacher and a policeman in Vineyard Town, Kingston. My poor eyesight hampered my academic growth. It was my teacher from Franklyn Town Primary who realized that I was being afflicted by my poor eyesight. Before that intervention, which led to me wearing spectacles, I was almost last in my class. After getting glasses, I moved to the top of the class and stayed there.

I attended the University of the West Indies (UWI), and the Royal University of Malta, but I believe my Excelsior High School years were really what defined me academically and has made me what I am today.

I spent the first two years studying medicine at the UWI before going to Malta, where I did the clinical aspect of my training to become a doctor. I finished in 1969. After that, I went to London, England, and continued my studies.

Back in Jamaica, in 1992, I was appointed Professor of Biochemistry and in 1993, I founded the University Diabetes Outreach Programme (UDOP), which now hosts the largest annual international diabetes conference in the Caribbean region. I have served as Vice Chairman, Chairman and country representative of the North American Region (NAR) of the International Diabetes Federation (IDF). The IDF is a worldwide alliance of over 200 diabetes associations in more than 160 countries. It represents more than estimated 170 million persons worldwide. (1994-97, Chairman for 1997-2000, and Country representative of the NAR from 2000-2003).

From June 2005 to December 2006, I was seconded as President & Chief Executive Officer of Blue Cross of Jamaica Limited. Also, in 2006, I was the recipient of the Queen Elizabeth II Gold Medal, Royal Society for the Promotion of Health, United Kingdom.

I have over 200 publications in peer reviewed journals, 7 books, 2 textbooks and numerous monograms.

March 2007 I was appointed to the post of President of the University of Technology (UTech) it has been stated that under my leadership, access and quality have grown in tandem, improving the lot of thousands of students who now have a greater number of options for higher learning."

I am married with eight beautiful daughters and I enjoy reading and public speaking.

My favorite quotation from Aristotle:
"We are, what we repeatedly do… Excellence then, is not an act, but a habit"

JAMAICAN EDUCATION/LITERARY TRIVIA 4

I was headmaster at Kinston College (KC), from the mid 1950's to 1971 when I resigned. Most of my former students who attended school during my administration were grateful to be afforded a sound education, including music. They also benefitted from the strong humility trait that I possessed. I insisted that my teachers should be firm, but fair to students, but nonetheless, I was strict and did not hesitate to discipline my students. I was committed to "educate gentlemen, not rascals." I did my best to lay a solid foundation for the future growth of KC in education and sports.

JAMAICAN EDUCATION/LITERARY TRIVIA 5

I was the headmistress of St. Andrew High School for Girls from 1968 to 1974. Moving from the class room I was appointed to the Jamaican Senate in 1974, and was assigned to the Ministry of Education as a Parliamentary Secretary. I also served as Secretary General of the Jamaica Teachers Association from 1975 to 1985 during which time I lobbied hard for the welfare of the nation's teachers.

JAMAICAN EDUCATION/LITERARY TRIVIA 6

I was born in St. Ann in 1921 and was educated at Jamaica College.

I served as a founding member of the Board of Management of the National Library of Jamaica. I worked in the West India Reference Library for three years before going to the United Kingdom to study for my degree and to qualify as a Librarian.

I was one of the first Jamaicans to qualify as a professional Librarian and when I returned home I was appointed supervisor of the West India Reference Library then joined the staff at the Library of the University College of the West Indies, I held that position for 30 years before retiring in 1981.

As founding member of the Jamaica Library Association I served as its first Secretary.

1972–Appointed President of the Jamaica Library Association.

1976–Elected as President of the Association of Caribbean Universities, research and Institutional Libraries (ACURIL).

Though I have had a stellar career as Librarian, I am passionate about Bibliography, I am also a Poet and my work has been published in Focus, Caribbean Quarterly and other publications.

I have been known to have made an outstanding contribution to Librarianship and Historical Scholarship in Jamaica and the Caribbean.

I have been awarded a Gold Musgrave Medal for my distinguished eminence in the field of Librarianship and Historical Scholarship.

Officer of the Order of Distinction by the Government of Jamaica

Some of my Publications appeared in:

Jamaica (vol. 45 in the World of Bibliography series): Clio Press, 1984

Sources of West Indian Studies: a Supplementary list with particular reference manuscript sources. Inter-Documentation Company, 1983.

Manuscripts relating to Commonwealth Caribbean Countries in United States and Canadian repositories. Caribbean Universities Press, 1975, I died in 2007

JAMAICAN EDUCATION/LITERARY TRIVIA 7

We were two Catholic sisters and we were significantly involved in Jamaica's educational growth, I was the headmistress at Immaculate High School from 1963 to 1991. During my tenure I insisted on the stern discipline of my students, along with their educational development.

My counterpart played a major role in the education of delinquent youth, particularly in music. She has worked with students at Alpha Boys' School in Kingston, molding them into prominent musicians in the ska and reggae genre. Her students included tenor saxophonist, Tommy McCook, trombonist, Don Drummond and trumpeter, Johnny "Dizzy" Moore, who went on to become members of the Skatalites. Her slight frame belied her no-nonsense disciplinarian approach, turning wayward young men through education into productive citizens. All her students were extremely appreciative of the guidance she gave. Although she never played a musical instrument, because of the musicians she produced from Alpha she was very influential in the development of Jamaican music.

JAMAICAN EDUCATION/LITERARY TRIVIA 8

I have been considered an 'all-rounder' in Jamaica's educational development. I taught at Calabar and Excelsior High schools, lectured at the Department of Education University of the West Indies, (UWI), served as Principal of Mico Training College (1972-80), and was Permanent Secretary in the Ministry of Education (1974-75), and President of the Jamaica Teacher's Association (1984-89). My commitment to the positive growth of teacher education was fulfilled with my appointment as Professor of Teacher Education at UWI. In 2008 I was elevated to the position of Chancellor of the Mico University College in Jamaica.

JAMAICAN EDUCATION/LITERARY TRIVIA 9

I was a prominent JLP MP and represented Northwest Clarendon from 1949 to 1983, and served as Minister of Education before independence, and became the first Minister of Education in independent Jamaica. My legacy was the 'New Deal in Education' introduced in 1965, which ensured that children from poor families had access to secondary education. I introduced the concept of the comprehensive high school; therefore, Jamaican students had easier access from primary to secondary education.

I also implemented a policy that reserved 70 per cent of the free places to secondary schools for students from primary schools who were successful in passing the minimum standard in the Common Entrance Examination (CEE); the remaining 30 per cent was allotted to students from private schools. Under an agreement with the World Bank I had 50 new secondary schools and 40 primary schools built by the end of 1967 and increased trained teachers from 350 to 1,000 by 1969. Though I have gone to rest, I have made an indelible mark in the educational system in Jamaica; a high school in Clarendon bares my name.

Who Am I?

Religion & Philantrophy

JAMAICAN RELIGION/HUMANITARIAN TRIVIA 1

I was born on March 08, 1912 to Frank and Rebecca. After my Primary Education I attended Tutorial Secondary and Commercial College and found later that my secretarial skills would help shape my future. After gaining some solid experience I became private secretary to one of Jamaica's prominent leaders until he became Prime Minister of Jamaica.

1962–September 7, (the month after Jamaica gained its independence), I became the 1st 'First Lady of Jamaica.'

I had a passion for children born to 'Destitute Parents.' I was Patron for the Bustamante Hospital for Children.

I have been presented with a number of awards:

1979–Golden Orchid Award from Venezuelan Government in recognition of dedication to Sir Alexander Bustamante's ideals.

1982–Order of Jamaica.

1983–Gleaner Company's Special Merit Award for Outstanding Service to the Nation.

1985–Trophy in Recognition of *Widow Exemplary Family Life* by Harmony in the Homes Movement.

1976 -1986–I received a plaque for Outstanding Public Service to Jamaica to mark the end of United Nations Decade of Women.

Long Service Award from Bustamante Hospital for Children for 21 years of Service.

Proclamation for the City of Opalocka for determination and commitment to the betterment of humankind, December 10, 1988 was declared 'My Day' (Dade County, Fl).

1988–Recognition for Work and Dedication from Friends of the Poor Incorporated, Florida & Woman's Inc.'s Celebration of Womanhood Award.

1990–Certificate of Recognition of National Day of Jamaica.

After living a full life I went to rest on Saturday July 25, 2009. I was ninety-seven years old.

JAMAICAN RELIGION/HUMANITARIAN TRIVIA 2

I was born on July 31, 1919 to Wilfred and Marie. After filling several roles in the Educational arena, I answered the call on my life and pursued studies in Theology after which I was ordained.

1960 -1974–Chairman Fort Augusta Prison Visiting Committee.

1960 -1965–Member of the Executive Committee of the Jamaica Mental Health Association.

1962–Editor-in-chief Mental Health Conference Report.

1965 - 1966–Chairman Ministry of Education Committee on Organization and Structure of Educational Systems.

1968–Chairman of Holy Trinity Secondary Board.

1973–Chairman of the Conference of Churches–I was elected at the Inaugural Meeting as the Chairman.

1996–Doctor of Divinity (D.D.) from Bethany College, Bethany, U.S.A.

I was the FIRST:

Headmaster of Campion College;

Jamaican Rector of St. George's College;

Jamaican Roman Catholic Bishop of Jamaica.

I developed a passion to serve mankind from an early age. I worked relentlessly in the inner city communities to spread the Eucharist of Love. My motto was "That all may be one". I retired November 11, 1994 and died September 3, 2002.

JAMAICAN RELIGION/HUMANITARIAN TRIVIA 3

I was 15 years old in 1953 and that was when I committed my life to Christ, I have never looked back. I attended Henderson High School (now York Castle), the College of Arts, Science and Technology (now, UTech) and at Denver Conservative Baptist Seminary in the USA, where I received the MA degree in Theology.

At 18 years old my passion for the gospel overtook all else and has dominated my life ever since. My working career ended by the time I was 31 years old as I was restless until I answered God's call to full time Christian Ministry.

A Dale Carnegie course on "How to win friends and influence people" made me discover my rhetorical capabilities and my love for the gospel-in Biblical parlance-my spiritual gift, nurtured by opportunities in Youth for Christ and my home church, Bethel Baptist, as well as several Christian Brethren assemblies, led to my fast pulpit maturation.

1969-I answered God's call institutionally to become Director of Jamaica Youth for Christ, (YFC), struggling there to survive in its 21st year of operations, following the sudden death of its youthful previous leader, Neville Witter.

1973 & 1980-I was asked to be Chairman of Billy Graham Evangelistic Crusaders conducted in Jamaica. For more than 16 years I was executive director of Jamaica YFC, moving it from three centers to being an island wide witness in 1985 I became Caribbean Director, while being recognized as the Americas Area Director for YFC International. I was a founding member of the National Prayer Breakfast.

1990-I was elected World Head of YFC International-president and chief executive officer-the first non-American or Third World person to hold that position since the organization was founded in the USA in 1945.

1994-The Caribbean Graduate School of Theology (CGST) conferred on me an honorary doctorate.

2000-The Billy Graham Evangelistic Association brought together the greatest assemblage of evangelists in the world from nearly 200 countries for AMSTERDAM 2000, held in the Netherlands. At that historic conference I was one of the select 15 speakers chosen to give keynote addresses.

2007-After 51 years of service, I officially retired as senior pastor of the Metropolitan Baptist Church in South Florida, but I have no plans of slowing down. In fact, I seem to be preaching far more now, than when I was a full time pastor. I am married to Sonia and we have 2 daughters.

Who Am I?

Business, Tourism & Law

Dunn's River Falls in Oco Rios

JAMAICAN BUSINESS/TOURISM/LAW TRIVIA 1

I was born in Jamaica on July 6, 1941. My mother had a little business as a dealer for appliances, and I used to go and help her. I loved it. I used to catch fish and sell them as a 12-year-old, and between fishing I used to love being in the shop with her.

In 1968 I worked hard and saved $3,000, with a goal to start in the appliance business then I realized Fedders air conditioners were not represented in Jamaica. I bought an airplane ticket and I headed to Edison, New Jersey. I met with the president's nephew. We really hit it off. He said to the finance people, "Look, he's paying cash for the first shipment, so there's nothing to lose; give him a chance."

I have never looked back since, today, that company, ATL Group, is also in the office equipment business, we are the distributor for Honda motorcars, and we have a newspaper called The Jamaica Observer.

I am a Jamaican businessman and the owner or Chairman of several businesses throughout the Caribbean, North America and Great Britain, my son Adam serves as CEO.

I own the chain of hotels named Sandals Resorts and Beaches Family Resorts. The Sandals resorts have repeatedly been awarded for their excellence in service. From its small beginnings, Sandals, based in Montego Bay, has grown into a multibillion-dollar company. Sandals Resorts International currently gives active support to more than 150 major projects in its host communities, through the company's philanthropic arm, The Sandals Foundation. This support ranges from the building of schools to the paying of teachers, to providing hospitals with linens, to bringing health care to the doorsteps of those who cannot afford it in Jamaica.

In former years I was also a major shareholder and chairman of Jamaica's national airline, Air Jamaica. I am dedicated to the progress of Jamaica, especially in the area of tourism and viable business development.

Among a host of awards, I was also the recipient of Caribbean World Magazine's Lifetime Achievement Award for my work in Jamaica, and has been called one of Jamaica's most-admired businessmen, by Kamal King, President of Cambridge College and Community Services.

I have inspired millions throughout the Caribbean region and the Diaspora, by helping to lay the foundation for their own success and touting the benefits of hard work and opportunity.

JAMAICAN BUSINESS/TOURISM/LAW TRIVIA 2

For more than 30 years I have been a steady force for many of the Caribbean's most visible travel brands, including the country of Jamaica, its national airline, Air Jamaica, Ltd., Sandals Resorts, Beaches Resorts and the Royal Plantation group of luxury boutique resorts. Rising from the tour business, I have become one of the Caribbean's most influential and sought-after experts and a critical player in bringing worldwide attention and ultimately visitors, to the region I know so well.

I began my travel career as a sales representative with the Jamaica Tourist Board (JTB), at the Kingston and Montego Bay offices. I later left the JTB and became general manager of J.A.M., a Jamaica-based tour company. Through partnerships with Intercontinental Hotels and the Maritz Travel Company, I rapidly expanded J.A.M., making it one of Jamaica's leading ground transportation companies at that time and a precursor of today's destination management companies.

I returned to the fourteen year association with the Jamaica Tourist Board. I joined as senior manager, was promoted to regional manager based in Chicago, and ultimately became deputy director of tourism, responsible for sales and marketing worldwide. Spurred on by the award-winning 'Come Back to Jamaica' campaign that significantly increased visitor arrivals during my tenure.

In 1992 I joined Sandals Resorts as executive vice president of sales worldwide. From my Miami office, I was responsible for public relations, sales promotions, and group sales for all Sandals Resorts brands worldwide and has been an integral part of the company's aggressive expansion beyond Jamaica that now includes Antigua, Turks and Caicos, Nassau and St. Lucia. For Sandals, I created the now trademarked WeddingMoon™ concept that combines a wedding and honeymoon and that has become synonymous with the destination wedding trend.

For ten years, I was an active member of the Board of Directors of Air Jamaica, Ltd., the national carrier of Jamaica. There, I was instrumental in the airline's significant rebranding in 1993 and consequent route expansion that brought more flights to Jamaica from more cities around the world.

Currently, I am the third vice president of the Caribbean Hotel Association (CHA), chairing its influential marketing committee and sits on the board of directors for the Caribbean Tourism Development Corporation (CTDC), a coming together of the Caribbean's most influential tourism entities: the Caribbean Hotel Association and the Caribbean Tourism Organization. I was Chairman of the Jamaica Tourist Board from 2007 - 2011 and Director of Tourism since 2008.

JAMAICAN BUSINESS/TOURISM/LAW TRIVIA 3

I was born in Bog Walk, St. Catherine on December 5, 1937, son of Leonard and Florence. I grew up in a business environment as my father was a seasoned businessman. I was Educated at Wolmer's Boys School.

In 1988, I founded LASCO, initially to package skimmed milk powder. The company has grown from a packager and distributor of a single product to a vast corporate entity, which provides hundreds of pharmaceuticals, food, household and personal care products to Jamaica, the Caribbean, Latin America, North America, and England.

In my quest to find nutritious, tasty, and affordable products for the Caribbean population, my extensive research led me to Solae Incorporated, a subsidiary of the prestigious Dupont Group. LASCO pioneered a range of products which utilized soy protein isolate and delivered to the consumer a highly nutritious product at an incredible low price.

The popularity of this product has made LASCO the Number One customer in the world for soy protein isolate from Solae Incorporated. Additionally, the American Soybean Association has hailed the LASCO Food Drink line as the tastiest soy product in the world.

Bolstered by this success, LASCO continues its global search for the most affordable, best quality products and have branded corned beef from Argentina, mackerel from Chile, ketchup from the Eastern Caribbean, and vitamins from an outstanding US supplier, whole milk from Ireland, and Corn Flakes from Germany.

1992–I received order of Distinction in the rank of Commander for outstanding services to Industry and Commerce in Jamaica. Also in that same year the 'Administrator of the Year' award was conferred on me by the Administrative Management Society, Jamaica Chapter.

2001–I received the second highest civilian Jamaican recognition, the Order of Jamaica, for my contribution to the development of business and my philanthropy. Also in 2001, I was named Jamaica Business Leader of the Year; I was one of the top nominees in the Ernst and Young Caribbean Entrepreneurship Awards and have been cited by the Jamaica Exporters Association, and the Jamaica Chamber of Commerce as an outstanding entrepreneur.

On April 2, 2001–LASCO Distributors formed an important alliance with Johnson & Johnson (Jamaica) Limited, as a result of that arrangement, Lasco Distributors handles the distribution of all Johnson & Johnson products in Jamaica.

I am divorced with 2 boys and 3 girls.

JAMAICAN BUSINESS/TOURISM/LAW TRIVIA 4

I was born in St. Mary, Middlesex, Jamaica, and graduated from Marymount High School in Highgate. I worked for Air Jamaica while studying for my Bachelor's degree. I received my Bachelor's degree in Business Management from the University of the West Indies in Mona, Jamaica, in 1991. Following college, I launched and managed six businesses, including a real estate development firm, a transportation company, a venture capital operation, and a banana exporting farm.

I received my Master's degree in Business Administration from Nova Southeastern University's H. Wayne Huizenga School of Business and Entrepreneurship in Florida.

I visited a bill-payment facility in Florida in the early 90s which led me to map out a template for Paymaster, the company I had planned to launch in Jamaica.

In October 1994, I founded Paymaster (Jamaica) Limited, consolidated bill payment agency and the first multi-transaction agency in the Caribbean, boasting more than 1.4 million customers and more than $40 billion in annual transactions, providing employment for over 400 people.

1997–I landed a contract with Jamaica Public Service (JPS).

2003–I became chairperson of the Tourism Product Development Company.

January 2009, I was privileged to witness with my daughter Morgan, the inauguration of President Barack Obama.

May 2010–I was appointed Jamaica's Ambassador to the United States, (the first female Jamaican Ambassador to the United States).

I took over as Jamaica's representative to the Organization of American States, and serves as Deputy Chairman of the Urban Development Corporation, Chairman of the Central Wastewater Treatment Company Limited, Director of the Board of RBTT Securities Jamaica Limited, Jamaica Trade and Investment, National Health Fund and the University of the West Indies' Mona School of Business. I am also the first female president of the American Chamber of Commerce of Jamaica.

I am proud to be a Jamaican and we know there is nowhere in the world like Jamaica, therefore it is worth the sacrifice to mentor, support and celebrate each other.

I am married to an electrical engineering consultant and we are blessed with two wonderful daughters.

JAMAICAN BUSINESS/TOURISM/LAW TRIVIA 5

I am President & CEO and Co-Founder of the nation's largest Caribbean franchise chain. We are a family-operated business with over 120 restaurants in nine states. We have consistently brought food lovers a taste of the Caribbean for over twenty years through the franchises and Jamaican patties being sold in grocery stores throughout the East Coast. We are coming from a small Jamaican village to the pinnacle of American Enterprise.

My new book, "The Baker's Son," tells the true story of an immigrant family from rural Jamaica who relocated to Bronx New York in the 1980s and overcame several major crises to achieve the American dream.

I have enjoyed an outstanding career, and have been bestowed with many awards for my entrepreneurial prowess and philanthropy. Most notable achievements include the prestigious Ernst & Young Entrepreneur of the Year Award, the Jamaica Observer's Business Leader Award, an Honorary Doctor of Letters from Medgar Evers College and the Order of Distinction from Jamaica. In 2005, I established the Mavis & Ephraim Hawthorne Scholarship Foundation, which has awarded numerous scholarships to young people both in the United States and Jamaica. I also serve as a director of the Caribbean American Chamber of Commerce and Industry and as Chairman of the Partnership Board of the American Foundation for the University of the West Indies.

Our company has partnered with Wisynco and Bigga Soft Drinks, which controls 70 per cent of the flavoured soft drinks market in Jamaica, and is seeking to position the product as the authentic "Made In Jamaica" carbonated drink of choice in North America. The Wisynco executive stated: "We chose this company to assist in our plan because, not only do they have extensive distribution along the east coast of the United States, they also cater to a vast Jamaican Diaspora and they also share similar value system of "making the lives of our people better." Wisynco was founded in 1965, and is one of Jamaica's oldest family-businesses and is among the country's largest distributors of consumer brands.

If you are interested in pursuing entrepreneurship, my secrets are shared in *The Baker's Son,* in the chapter entitled "Wealth."

However, I attribute the real source of my success in business to my wife, siblings, and children and to the deep Christian faith inculcated in me by my parents from a young age.

JAMAICAN BUSINESS/TOURISM/LAW TRIVIA 6

I was born on May 5, 1940 to Eric and Lucille.

I attended Jamaica College, The University of the West Indies, Mona (UWI), and Oxford University.

During my studies at the University of the West Indies, I represented the University Students Conference in Europe and the Middle East.

I was the second West Indian to become President of the Oxford Union.

I was the first black TV reporter at BBC.

1970–I became the youngest Jamaican to have been appointed Director of Tourism, one month before my thirtieth birthday.

1970 - 1974–I was the Founding Executive Director of the Private Sector Organization of Jamaica.

1974 - 1976–I became the Chairman of the Jamaica Hotel School.

1977 - 1978–I became a member of the Jamaica Senate.

1978 - 1979–I became the Director Multi-National Tourism Program of the Organization of American States (OAS).

1989-1990–I was a Contributing Journalist to the Jamaica Herald.

OTHER ACHIEVEMENTS:

Director of Air Jamaica,

Member of Parliament, Eastern Portland, Minister of Tourism – JLP,

Minister of Information – JLP,

Member of the Jamaica Government Air Policy Committee,

Member of the Public Passenger Transport Board,

I enjoy squash, swimming and tennis during my spare time...

JAMAICAN BUSINESS/TOURISM/LAW TRIVIA 7

I was born on July 26, 1931 to Wadie and Angel.

I believe I was destined to be in Law from my early years. I was called to the Bar and was admitted to practice and appointed Clerk of Courts; I became Acting Registered Magistrate for St. Catherine and also Registered Magistrate for St. Mary and St. James

1965 - 1968–I became Registered Magistrate for St. Andrew

1985–I was sworn in as Chief Justice of Jamaica by Sir Florizel Glaspole at Kings House where I pledged to carry out my duties without partiality, fear or favor.

1992–Accepted by United Kingdom Privy Council on September 1, 1992. I was the fourth Caribbean Chief Justice to be appointed to the Privy Council and the first from Jamaica.

1996–I retired on July 25, 1996 after giving thirty eight years in the judicial service.

I am married to Hope and we have two children

I enjoy all types of outdoor sports

Who Am I?

Beauty & Fashion

Taylor Davis–young Jamaican beauty

JAMAICAN BEAUTY/FASHION TRIVIA 1

I was the first Jamaican to be crowned Miss World. I was 20-year-old, five-feet three-inches tall. I was short by Miss World standards, but I made history by being the first person from my country to take home the coveted Miss World title. November 7, 1963 was one year and three months after Jamaica became an independent nation.

The pageant was held in London, England and it was an experience I will never forget.

When I entered the competition it was quite a job at the time to get permission from my father to be in a beauty contest. Back then the Miss Jamaica Beauty Pageant was run by the Jamaica Junior Chamber of Commerce. At the time a member of the chamber encouraged me to enter the contest.

After the crowning and celebrations in London I returned to Jamaica to an amazing reception. The airport was filled with people welcoming me. The Government had issued three million commemorative stamps with my picture in my swimsuit on it. There were receptions with Sir Alexander Bustamente and Governor General Sir Clifford Campbell and his wife. I was presented with the gold key to the city of Kingston.

The Miss World contest has changed over the years, for example when I entered there were only 40 countries participating. Today more than 116 countries enter each year, but there is great value in the competition.

I think it is of great benefit to a country when their contestant wins the Miss World crown. She immediately becomes a goodwill ambassador, travelling the world and promoting her country.

I am proud to be a Jamaican and even though I currently live in Canada a part of me will always be in Jamaica.

JAMAICAN BEAUTY/FASHION TRIVIA 2

I was born September 8, 1985 and was crowned Miss Jamaica World 2007 beauty pageant, as well as the 2010 Miss Jamaica Universe pageant. I represented Jamaica at the Miss World 2007 contest held in Sanya, China and at Miss Universe 2010 held at the Mandalay Bay Resort and Casino, Las Vegas, Nevada, U.S. on August 23, 2010, where I finished as the first runner up to Ximena Navarrete of Mexico.

I was 1st runner-up in Miss World Beach Beauty and a finalist in the Miss World Sports, Miss World Talent, Miss World Top Model and the 'Beauty with a Purpose' Award. During the telecast, I made the final top 16.

In the Miss Universe 2010 pageant in Las Vegas on August 2010 I scored the highest in swimsuit and came in second in evening gown. My measurements were: 34-25-36.

I currently hold a bachelor's degree of fine arts with a concentration in dance from the State University of New York at Brockport and a Master's degree in Recreation and Leisure Management. After the Miss Universe pageant, I appeared in an American ad campaign for the car brand Toyota; I also appeared in commercials for Pepsi Refresh in the US and the Sprite campaign in India. I have also appeared in publications such as Skywritings magazine, Caribbean Beat magazine, Woman & Home, Fair Lady, Buzz, Collage, Soul, Basia and Ocean Style. I have also hosted Digicel Rising Stars.

JAMAICAN BEAUTY/FASHION TRIVIA 3

I was voted Miss Jamaica in 1973 and as I left to represent Jamaica in the Miss World Pageant later that year I felt proud to be a Jamaican. I was placed 3rd in the Miss World Pageant, however the title was withdrawn from the winner and the runner-up was unable to serve, I represented Miss World for the remainder of the year. It was an experience of a lifetime.

JAMAICAN BEAUTY/FASHION TRIVIA 4

I was born October 24, 1954 in Toronto, Canada, to a Jamaican father and a Canadian mother. I have 2 brothers.

I moved to Jamaica when I was only four years old, and attended the Immaculate Conception Academy. As a teenager I began participating in beauty pageants, including Miss Jamaica Body Beautiful and Miss Universe Bikini. I was invited to participate in the Miss World competition in 1976; I traveled to London and won the title on November 19th, 1976, becoming the second Jamaican to do so.

Two years after I won the Miss World title I had another big event in my life; I gave birth to a rising star; a Grammy winning reggae musician, born in 1978. His father was an international reggae artist and a few of the songs he wrote was based on our relationship.

Three years later I married senator and attorney-at-law Tom Tavares-Finson in 1981 with whom I have a son, Christian, born in 1982 and a daughter Leah, born in 1986. We divorced in 1995.

2012 London Olympics: As I watched the Jamaican Team claim their medals and made Jamaica proud, I remember how it felt to claim the crown for Jamaica back in 1976. I will go to my grave feeling that this was one of the best experiences of my life.

As a supportive mother I proudly watched my son perform for the Jamaica 50 celebrations at the O2 arena while in London. At 57-years-young, I am currently working as an interior designer. However, I am still a fitness enthusiast, going to the gym as often as possible. But that might be because I have to keep up with my three grandchildren with a fourth expected in October.

I am currently married to musician Rupert Bent II and I have been pursuing my career as a Recording Artist and Entrepreneur. I founded a Rastafarian craft store called "Ital Craft" in Jamaica.

JAMAICAN BEAUTY/FASHION TRIVIA 5

I was born on August 27, 1975 to parents Rene and Dorothy and grew up in Retreat, St. Mary, Jamaica. My father was a farmer and my mother, a hairdresser.

I became head girl at Queens High School and immediately following graduation I entered the Miss Jamaica Beauty Pageant, after winning that title I gained entry to the Miss World pageant, held on November 27, 1993 at the Sun City Entertainment Centre in Sun City, South Africa.

This was the 43rd Miss World Pageant and it attracted 81 contestants from all over the world. It was also the second consecutive staging of the pageant in Sun City. The event was hosted by actor and future James Bond Pierce Brosnan.

At 18 years old, five feet seven inches tall I won the Miss World title and was crowned in a singing and dancing extravaganza. I became the third Jamaican to be crowned Miss World.

Today, I am a politician in Jamaica and I will always be proud of achieving the Miss World title in 1993.

JAMAICAN BEAUTY/FASHION TRIVIA 6

I was the designer of choice for several fashion conscious Jamaican women. I was hailed as the "First Lady of Jamaican Fashion." It was said I designed the fashions for more Miss Jamaica beauty contestants than any other designers. Joan Crawford (Miss World 1962), and Mitzie Constantine (Miss Jamaica 1964) wore my designs.

My exquisite ball gowns graced ladies at every state occasion, and several brides also wore my famous creations during my 60-year career. Remarkably, on my death bed, I disclosed that I had no formal training in fashion designing, but you would never have guessed.

JAMAICAN BEAUTY/FASHION TRIVIA 7

I am director of my own Fashion Designing Company and I received formal training in New York and I also gained experience in the New York Fashion district. I also designed fashion for notable Jamaican women and beauty queens, including Miss World, Cindy Breakspeare. During my career, I served as president of the Jamaica Designers Association, and was contracted by Air Jamaica to coordinate the airline's in-flight fashion shows during the earlier years of Air Jamaica.

JAMAICAN BEAUTY/FASHION TRIVIA 8

I was famous for designing practical wear for Jamaican men in the 1970's. When I created the 'Kariba' for then Prime Minister Michael Manley, I started a fashion revolution. Men rushed to my St. Andrew shop to order the then popular bush jackets and Kariba (bush jackets and pants made from the same type and color material). I designed versions of the kariba, suitable for office, casual and formal wear. Jackets and ties were a rarity in the 1970's, as bush jackets and the kariba were more practical wear for men in the Jamaican climate, but when Manley went out of politics in the 1980s so did the bush jacket and the kariba, as some saw the garments associated with the philosophy of Democratic Socialism.

Who Am I?
Aviation & Agriculture

JAMAICAN AVIATION/AGRICULTURE TRIVIA 1

I was born in Kingston and migrated to the US, Miami's inner city with my parents when I was only six years old.

I always had a love for aviation and at the age of 15, I was inspired by another Jamaican pilot, Gary Robinson. I set out to not only master the field of Aviation but also to become an inspiration to other youth. I was accustomed to seeing teens develop into nothingness, with not much confidence in their future or hope for substantial progress after high school. During my high school years there was very little incentive for me or my classmates to get off the streets and pursue real careers. And the situation hasn't improved; in the neighborhoods between my home and high school, more than 24 kids under the age of 21 were murdered by other kids under 21 in a twelve month period.

I had a dream to fly around the world but I was too young and I had no money, but that did not stop me. Through my non-profit organization, 'Experience Aviation' and being an aerospace student I was able to build my plane with $300,000 worth of donated parts. I encountered snowstorms, sandstorms, monsoons and even hurricanes, I began my mission on March 23, 2007 and returned safely on June 26, 2007, history was created.

I was the youngest and first black person to fly solo around the world and I was able to undertake this mission because of my strong faith in God. I feel my ability to motivate countless young people to pursue careers in aviation is my actual purpose on earth. I feel that aviation has chosen me for this purpose.

My organization aims at encouraging kids to pursue careers in aviation and aerospace. Citing statistics that show a shortage in qualified aviation industry personnel over the next 10 years, I have developed a plan to foster the interests of youth by informing them of the procedures to get the necessary training and by promoting confidence in their potential.

I was told I was too young, I was told I didn't have enough money and that I couldn't do this, I was told that I didn't have the wisdom, the strength or the experience. I was told I would never come back home. But despite all that, on June 26, 2007, as I taxied my plane upon arrival at the Opa-locka airport, Miami Florida, the Miami Dade Fire Dept fire trucks shot water cannons and the crowd cheered as I made a safe landing home.

JAMAICAN AVIATION/AGRICULTURE TRIVIA 2

Growing up in Montego Bay, I would often watch the planes take off from the Montego Bay Airport, and I yearned for the day when I would fly. Drive and determination kept me going and I did not stop until I reached the captainship in 1996.

I was one of the first women in the Western Hemisphere to become a commercial jet airline pilot when I was hired by Air Jamaica as a second officer in 1979.

I was also the first female captain on Air Jamaica in 1986 and the first on an all-female flight in 1997, consisting of six women.

I am currently working with Atlas Air Inc in New York.

I love flying, I love it! It's in my blood. It's in my nature. My husband is also an airline pilot. We love it. It started when I was very young and my mom took me for my first flight.

My husband Brian did 21 years with Air Jamaica, 10 years as captain at the Jamaica Defence Force Air Wing and has been with JetBlue as a captain for the past seven years.

He admitted that while he was attracted to me as a pilot, it was really my mind that had him hooked.

My interest in flying started at age five when I took my first flight.

This passion was further piqued when I started working with Air Jamaica as a flight attendant in 1974. In March 1975, I took an introductory flight at Wings Jamaica Ltd and commenced flying lessons, earning my private pilot license that December.

In 1977, I earned my Jamaican commercial license, I am the third woman to do so in Jamaica. Then in 1978 I worked part time at Rutair and Wings Jamaica Ltd as an instructor before joining Air Jamaica as a second officer in 1979.

I am a member of the International Society of Women Airline Pilots, the Ninety-Nines, Women in Aviation International, and the Aircraft Owners and Pilots Association.

I was awarded for my outstanding contribution to the development of aviation in Jamaica by the Jamaica Civil Aviation Authority as it celebrated 100 years of powered flights.

JAMAICAN AVIATION/AGRICULTURE TRIVIA 3

I was born on December 31, 1904.

1970–I was the first recipient of the Norman Manley Award for Excellence (My field being Agriculture focusing on Cattle).

1971–Doctor of Science (Honoris causa), University of the West Indies.

1978–I was awarded, 'Order of Merit,' by the Government of Jamaica for work of national and international importance.

1987–I received the Mutual Security Foundation Outstanding Achievement Award.

1989–Fellow of the Jamaican Society for Agricultural Sciences.

1992–I was inducted into the Professional Societies Association in Jamaica.

1994–I published my autobiography titled *Cattle and I.*

My extensive research resulted in the first breed of indigenous Jamaican cattle, 'The Jamaican Hope,' which I used as the basis for my Ph.D. thesis at Edinburgh University, Scotland. To this day I remain a role model for many Jamaican scientists. I died in 1994 at the age of 90.

What Place or Town Am I?

Fort Charles, Port Royal. Photograph courtesy of the Jamaica Tourist Board.
All stories in this segment provided by the Jamaica Tourist Board

JAMAICAN TOWN/PLACE TRIVIA 1

My rich history dates back to 1534, I was made the capital of Jamaica and called Villa de la Vega (city on the plains). In 1655, I remained the capital of Jamaica and was renamed St Jago de la Vega, I served as the capital under the English for 217 years. Although none of the original buildings remain–most were destroyed during the British invasion while others toppled during the 1692 earthquake–there is still a subtle influence of my origin alive in the city. Today, I am one of the oldest continuously occupied places in the Western hemisphere. As Jamaica's third largest urban centre, a visit to my town reveals an interesting mix of a bygone era and modern city life.

The Rodney Memorial, created by renowned sculptor John Bacon in honor of Admiral George Rodney, a key player in the successful British defense of the island from French invaders, was "kidnapped" in 1876 by the city of Kingston when I ceased to be the capital. Irate residents of my town argued their case through the correct channels, but their protests fell on deaf ears, until one day the statue was removed from Kingston and returned by force to its original home. In the process, the statue lost an arm, but is still loved dearly by my residents, as this statue is an integral part of my heritage and aesthetic.

My town square, offers fantastic representations of 18th-and 19th-century architecture. Emancipation Square, offers a colorful glimpse into the island's past. You'll find fascinating buildings such as the Town's Cathedral–the oldest Anglican Cathedral in the Caribbean–and the Phillipo Baptist Church. A recent archaeological digging in my town resulted in the uncovering of a Jewish synagogue, originally constructed in 1704. The building is believed to have been one of two worship centers for Spanish and Portuguese Jews fleeing the Spanish Inquisition.

I am proud of my history and I invite Jamaicans from around the world to visit my town and get acquainted with the rich heritage and experience the stunning examples of Georgian Architecture. There is a lot to discover and so much more to learn.

JAMAICAN TOWN/PLACE TRIVIA 2

I am one of the oldest and most historic regions of the country; I have maintained much of my independence as well as my heritage. I was once the enclave of pirates and other outlaws and I still have a strong seafaring tradition. Much of the old part of my city was described in the 17th century as the "wickedest city in the west." A section of me, lies underwater, the result of the 1692 earthquake that swallowed about two-thirds of the then-living space. Since then, another earthquake in 1907, numerous hurricanes, fires, and various population-decimating diseases have plagued me. Despite all the waters around me, I am a virtual archaeological gold mine, filled with pieces of history that tell of everyday life in the earliest days of English occupation. I am also home to the Archaeological Division of the Jamaica National Heritage Trust (JNHT), which recently completed a sonar survey of the underwater city, revealing a sunken pirate ship in the Kingston Harbor. To date thousands of artifacts have been recovered, and there are plans to develop a local museum to showcase these items once the research has been complete.

I am a community of proud people, fiercely defensive of our privacy, yet warm and welcoming to those interested in visiting. My community is especially close-knit because of its layout– everywhere is within walking distance, and there are several generations of people all living together. Perhaps my best attribute is my comfortable, laid-back temperament–on any given day there are children playing in the streets, young adults gathered in groups hanging out, and older folk sitting on verandas watching the world go by.

Be sure to stop by the Giddy House when you visit, the building was built in 1888 to house the artillery store for the fort. Visitors are allowed to enter the building; however, walking through the building wreaks havoc on the senses, creating a nauseating effect. The tour guides are warm and welcoming they will help to relax you and make you feel quite at home.

JAMAICAN TOWN/PLACE TRIVIA 3

I am sitting on 11 lush acres in the capital city, my stately mansion was once the home of Jamaica's first black millionaire, George Stiebel. Built in 1891, on what was originally a 51-acre property.

Visitors that come to see me can go back in time with a tour of the Georgian-style great house. Furnished with a collection of 19th century antiques from Jamaica and the Caribbean region, I tell the tale of privileged West Indian society in the Victorian Era. The ballroom still has the original English chandelier purchased by Stiebel for the room.

The finely crafted, wooden Great House is even more remarkable given that it was constructed by a man whose background made his climb to success particularly difficult. George Stiebel, the son of a black housekeeper and a German Jewish merchant, made his fortune from investments in gold mines in Venezuela. He purchased 99 properties in Jamaica, including this one.

Today, the old stables, kitchen and other buildings on the property host some of Jamaica's finest restaurants, confectioneries and souvenir shops. On Sundays, lovers hold hands and stroll across my manicured lawns, while families sit back and enjoy one of the best brands of ice-cream on the island.

If you have never stopped by to visit before, you owe it to yourself, come by and experience the difference.

JAMAICAN TOWN/PLACE TRIVIA 4

I am Jamaica's premier educational institution. I am the home to many attractions for the visitor and the student. I started out in 1948 as a College of the University of London, but I achieved full university status in 1962, the year we gained independence.

I invite you to take a walking tour of my campus. Stroll through the chapel with its gardens in full bloom, stop by on a Saturday afternoon and hear solemn vows being exchanged. Spend some time by the Aqueduct or the geology museum and you'll begin to appreciate the rich history surrounding this blessed island.

Some of Jamaica's best have given credit to the stellar educational system in place. My library occasionally host book signings of renowned authors.

There are so many sights to see and stories to tell that you need not take my word for it, but become more acquainted with this rock solid educational institutional for yourself.

JAMAICAN TOWN/PLACE TRIVIA 5

I am one of the largest and most important inland towns of St Ann, primarily because of the high concentration of educational institutions in the area as well as the large Farmer's Market. Just to the north of me is the Minard Estate, the pimento plantation and home of the eccentric and caustic owner, from whom the town is named. In the 19th century, he owned the twin estates of Minard and Huntley, and because of his wealth and clout in the area, he was instrumental in local politics. In the 19th century, he led a group called the Colonial Church Union, a coalition of Anglican congregants who would routinely persecute non-conformist missionaries and their followers by burning churches and free villages. For his efforts, he was honored with a monument in the Anglican churchyard. Ironically, the main thorn in the side of the Colonial Church Union at the time, Dr James Johnson's Jamaica Evangelistic Mission (known popularly as the Tabernacle Church), is today one of the institutions that residents are most proud of. My town is heralded as the birthplace of this movement, an offshoot of the Baptist Church, which today is one of the largest groups of churches in the island.

My town is also an important trading centre for local farmers who live in the surrounding Dry Harbor Mountains. Norman Market, one of the oldest in the island, was famous for the bells atop the steeple, which would ring on major holidays, echoing through the mountains and surrounding towns. Today, the market is in transition, having outgrown its original location, but is still the largest and most prosperous in the area, attracting sellers from as far away as St Elizabeth. Some of Jamaica's most respected educational institutions are located in and around me. These schools have longstanding reputations and alma mater lists that include some of the most prominent names in Jamaican society. One of the newer institutions, the Town's Community College, in just a few years has managed to make a name for itself with its rigorous and effective skills training and university preparatory programs.

In the 19th century, this area was home to many sugar and cattle estates and plantations, producing sugar, pimento and other crops. Today the legacy of the Colonial period remains, with many elegant homes scattered over the rolling hills and valleys around me. Many are privately owned, but most owners are proud of their properties and sometimes allow viewings if politely asked. Of note is the Minard Estate, now a cattle-breeding estate with the New Hope Great House, and the ruins of the Minard Great House. When in the area please look up Rev. Desmond Lloyd Smith and his beautiful wife, Mauva, they will welcome you with open arms and give you a taste of country living.

JAMAICAN TOWN/PLACE TRIVIA 6

I lie right between the border of St Andrew and St Thomas, coincidentally or not, beside me is the lesser-known sister bay, Cow Bay. It is said that both bays were so named because the whole area was once a slaughter centre in the days of the buccaneers and the early days of English Colonialism. I am an energetic, close-knit community, and at night, the coastline pulsates with rhythms from the various nightclubs that line the beach.

From the gate at Cane River Falls Park, the faint sound of rushing water gently beckons, and 101 steps down a steep narrow walkway, tucked behind huge boulders, is an unexpected find, the Cane River Falls. Although the falls are the closest and most easily accessible by residents of Kingston, the nation's capital, they are still relatively unknown, and on most days no more than a handful of people actually visit. The falls is just inland from me and it has been said that the falls was Reggae artist Bob Marley's favorite place to wash his dreadlocks.

I am also known as Nine Mile because of the distance from downtown Kingston. I house the largest settlement of Rastas on the island. The camp, located at 13 Marcus Garvey Way, Zion Hill, comprises the homes, prayer houses and meeting places of more than 300 Rastas, with separate units for men and women. Generally, the Rastas in the camp observe strict prayer rites at specified times, and at 6:00 a.m., 12:00 p.m. and 6:00 p.m. the chants and drumbeats can be heard from as far away as the coast.

Not far from my village, at the top of the Queensbury Ridge, is a monument to "Three-Finger" Jack Mansong, an 18th century "Robin Hood" character said to be associated with the region. Three-Finger Jack began his life as a slave on a nearby plantation, but in his adult life was labeled a rabble-rouser and was sentenced to death for inciting other slaves to rebellion. Jack cheated death and took to the hills, terrorizing the British authorities and landowners. The monument is strategically located in an area long known as "Three-Finger Jack Corner", a breathtaking lookout point that offers stunning views of the Caribbean Sea from between two small hills.

JAMAICAN TOWN/PLACE TRIVIA 7

Back in the 18th century I was a haven for runaway slaves. Many slaves survived because I provided a hiding place.

I am a natural hollowed-out place in the ground that is characterized by coastal limestone that is easily accessed. I feature a series of interconnected passageways and chambers, light holes, stalactites and stalagmites. My most striking features are the rock formations and the small grotto lake at the innermost cavern.

Take a deep breath; courage is required for entry and bravely journey through the walls of the unknown.

JAMAICAN TOWN/PLACE TRIVIA 8

Talk about Love, not only did they talk about it, they demonstrated it.

I am located east of Treasure Beach; I am a sheer 1600-foot cliff overhanging the sea.

Two slave lovers vowed never to be separated from each other and it was here that they jumped to their deaths together, rather than be apart.

Wow, some kind of love! Make it your business to visit my site and let the tour guides tell you the whole story. You will be in awe!

JAMAICAN TOWN/PLACE TRIVIA 9

I am a river that shares my name with the town. I am the main source of the water that irrigates the vast agricultural regions of the Clarendon plains, but is largely unnavigable and infested with crocodiles. I contain some of the most radioactive waters in the world. On average, my waters are a consistent 90 to 95 degrees Fahrenheit throughout the year, and contain high levels of magnesium, calcium, sulphate and natural chloride. My mineral waters flow directly from a source in a rock and are especially recommended for use by those suffering from rheumatism, arthritis, sciatica and nerve complaints. My waters are so hot and radioactive that patrons are warned to stay in for no more than ten to twenty minutes at a time, and then for no more than three baths per day.

Legend has it that a slave, owned by one Mr Jonathan Ludford of Clarendon, committed an offence for which he was brutally whipped and locked away in a dungeon. Imprisoned and severely wounded, and vowing never to be a slave again, he broke out of his chains and escaped. Days later, the man returned to the estate in full health, healed of the wounds he had received only a few days before. In an effort to convince others to run away with him, he told a tale of a remarkable salty spring in which he had bathed. Everyone who saw him was amazed at his recovery, and soon, word reached the owner of the estate who had ordered him punished. Ludford himself was astounded at the recovery, and promised to grant the slave freedom if he revealed the location of the spring. The slave led a party to the location, and Ludford promptly acquired the spring and the lands around it, and started the baths. Upon his death, Ludford bequeathed all the property and land to the government and people of Jamaica to benefit all who needed them. Since the first baths opened in 1794, thousands of people have visited me to heal themselves from a variety of ailments.

JAMAICAN TOWN/PLACE TRIVIA 10

I am the fast-growing commercial district that is increasingly becoming the business centre of Jamaica. I am built on lands formerly part of a park and race track. Major construction projects began in the late 1950s, and still continue today. I house most of Jamaica's modern multi-storied office blocks and financial institutions. I am the core of Jamaica's financial sector. By night, I become Kingston's playground, and the glamorously fashionable patrons of the numerous bars, nightclubs and restaurants replace stodgy suited professionals.

I offer visitors a chance to experience Jamaican history and culture. To the west is Devon House, a stately historic mansion with expansive, meticulously manicured lawns that has been converted to a museum with outlying craft shops and gourmet restaurants. On the southern end is Emancipation Park, one of the largest public green spaces in the city, with jogging trails, an amphitheatre and a mini-botanical garden. Dotted along the minor roads are numerous art galleries, shopping mall such as the Island Life Mall, and performing arts theatres such as The Barn Theatre, and The Little Theatre, home to the internationally acclaimed National Dance Theatre Company.

The northern section is lined with bars, lounges, nightclubs, restaurants and other entertainment hot spots. At night the street is filled with vendors and revellers moving from venue to venue, and the partying often does not stop until the next morning, when it is amusing to see diligent executives arriving to start their day, passing by straggling clubbers on their way home.

Right in the middle is the Asylum nightclub, the most popular disco in Kingston. Each week, Asylum has theme nights, of which two of the more exciting nights are Ladies' Night and Dancehall Night. Both are especially worth a night out on the town, but if clubbing is not your passion, join the throngs of onlookers and stand outside the club observing the patrons as they go inside. The outrageous hairstyles, fashions and vehicles of the men and women that come into the club are a spectacle all by themselves - sometimes amazing, or entertaining at the very least.

JAMAICAN TOWN/PLACE TRIVIA 11

I am a cast iron tower, painted red and white, 100-feet tall and 18-feet wide, built in 1841. I am the oldest one of its kind in Jamaica and certainly one of the more sturdy ones. I am located on the farthest tip of the island's east coast, I am the first point of impact from hurricanes, I have withstood the brute force of gale-force winds and high seas. West African workers who came to the island as indentured labourers from Sierra Leone, built me. As a result, the area is known for its strong retention of African customs and heritage–even today strains of African-influenced language, religion and settlement patterns have been recorded here.

My balcony provides a phenomenal view of the various cane pieces of the estate, the Blue Mountain range, the St Thomas coastline and the seemingly endless Caribbean Sea. West of me lies one of the most secluded yet spectacular beaches on the island, Holland Bay. The route to me and the beach is not direct, nor is it easily accessible. Do not attempt the journey in anything less than a very reliable vehicle, and be prepared to get lost in the cane fields.

Holland Bay, a large cove with a strong surf and powder-white sand, is certainly worth the trek through an unmarked cane area starting in Golden Grove. Most times, the beach is deserted and serene, with the only noises coming from me.

From my balcony you will have uninterrupted views of Jamaica's eastern coastline, the vast greenery of the sugar and banana plantations and the blue shadows of the Blue Mountain range are sure to dazzle and amaze. Do exercise caution ascending and descending the stairs; there are MANY of them, and they are somewhat steep. Please come by and visit.

JAMAICAN TOWN/PLACE TRIVIA 12

Fifteen minutes by boat from Port Royal is a small, low-lying island cay with one of the most beautiful beaches in Jamaica. The largest of the many small cays off the coast of Port Royal, I am uninhabitable by humans because I am occasionally submerged when the tide comes in. Unfortunately, I have been the source of many scams and hoaxes "sold" to unsuspecting buyers as a potential location for a private resort. Don't be fooled, I am a part of Jamaica, and the beaches are public and opened to all.

On Sundays, I am the favourite beach getaway for city folk, many of whom moor their boats at the Morgan's Harbour Marina and sail out for the afternoon with lunch and refreshments, since there are no facilities on the island. From Morgan's Harbour, a shuttle or boat rental for the day can be arranged, but for the intrepid visitors, a small fee will convince a fisherman in the town of Port Royal to offer a ride to the island in the morning and return in the evening.

On weekdays clothing-optional, sunbathing is acceptable as there is a possibility that there will be no one around. On Sundays, however, the tone and temperament changes completely, as the tiny island pulsates with life, laughter and good times.

Stop by and experience some of the best snorkeling on the south.

JAMAICAN TOWN/PLACE TRIVIA 13

I am a booming business centre set amidst rolling hills and lush vegetation. I am situated some 2000 feet above sea level, and is one of the more peaceful and attractive places on the island. I am the capital of a parish that was named after a Duke and later he named me after his son, way back in 1816. Wealthy English settlers and expatriates favored this part of the island, building impressive mansions and country homes because the landscape reminded them of their own countryside in climate, temperament and aesthetic. Today, a large number of the residents are Jamaicans who have lived abroad for many years, usually in England, and who have returned to retire.

The Court House is of particular interest, built in 1820 with limestone blocks cut by slave labor. The courthouse, one of only four original public buildings, has a portico supported by Doric columns flanked by a curving double staircase.

I am the home of Jamaica's first major bauxite mining facility and today it is a prosperous metropolis because of the mineral found in the blood-red soil. The process of excavating is a fascinating window into an important element of Jamaica's economy, and the West Indies Alumina Company, offers complete mine tours on appointment.

I have retained many characteristics of my Colonial heritage. One in particular, the English tradition of maintaining and nurturing complete gardens around fabulous mansions is still a favourite among residents. The most famous garden is that belonging to Mrs. Carmen Stephenson's. It's a delightful showcase of Jamaican flowers and an award-winning orchid greenhouse. Mrs. Stephenson is an active member of the Horticultural Society, the oldest of its kind in the Western hemisphere. In addition to maintaining her famous garden, she also runs a small flower shop in the Shopping Centre that is supplied by the garden. Most days, Mrs. Stephenson would be more than happy to chat for a few minutes about the variety she keeps in stock. Please stop by the shop or call ahead to make an appointment to see the famous garden.

JAMAICAN TOWN/PLACE TRIVIA 14

Did you know that I was the second town to be established in Jamaica by the colonizing Spaniards? Formerly I was a bustling seaport under both Spanish and English rule; today I reflect little of my former prosperity or importance. Except for a handful of buildings, not much remains of the Colonial-era architecture. I am set in the centre of a deep inlet of the northern coastline with a small island just offshore, and the bay is certainly one of the most picturesque in Jamaica. As capital to one of the fourteen parishes, I house the Courthouse, an old, elegant building subtly dominating the waterfront.

I have been known to have a very old and deep-seated tradition of protest. From as early as 1655, African slaves were set free when the fleeing Spanish took to the hills, forming Maroon communities and carrying out the occasional attack on British estates and towns. In 1760, Tacky, the notorious rebel slave, led a revolt against slave owners that lasted over a month before British authorities could suppress the fighting. Centuries later, in a 1938 riot that started in Islington, a small farming community nearby, four men died as a result of clashes with local police. The spirit of protest lives on, although in recent times not much has been able to incite the people here to mass violence.

In front of the courthouse is a monument to Tacky, a freedom fighter of the 18th century. In 1760 Tacky, an African slave assembled a guerrilla army to attack their British enslavers and seize control of the land. The revolt started on the nearby Frontier plantation, but spread quickly after Tacky and his followers raided the munitions store. Tacky's Revolt was one of the most pivotal slave uprisings in Jamaican history, because, although outnumbered and ill equipped, Tacky's followers kept the British at bay for more than a month before the rebellion could be subdued. Following the rebellion, many of the slaves that managed to evade the British banded together and fled to the hills to join the Maroons, but as many as 300 slaves were executed for their participation.

The Parish Church, built in 1861 of limestone blocks on the edge of the bay, is one of the most picturesque structures anywhere on the island. The modest chapel is set against the dazzling turquoise harbor, framed by tall palm trees whose leaves rustle gently in the warm sea breezes.

JAMAICAN TOWN/PLACE TRIVIA 15

I am the centre of downtown Kingston. Long before Kingston took over from Spanish Town as the island's capital city, I held significance as a centre of activity. When Kingston became the capital of the nation, I became somewhat of a public arena used for just about any imaginable purpose including public hangings and floggings. The wealthy and fashionable would also meet and greet in transit. To the north of me is the Ward Theatre, to the east lies Coke Methodist Church, the first Methodist chapel to be built in Jamaica, and to the west is the Coronation Market, the largest and most frequented market in the island. To the south stands the beautiful and historic Kingston Parish Church, with its many interesting graves, tributes and gifts from the wealthy citizens of the city. For many years the church stood as the major landmark in Kingston, giving rise to the phrase, "born under the clock" and a reference to Kingstonians born within sight or earshot of the Kingston Parish Church bell.

In 1870, after the Colonial Militia and the troops moved their base northwards to Up Park Camp, city officials petitioned to create a public green space for the city of Kingston. Upon completion, in true Colonial style, the British erected a statue of the monarch, Queen Victoria, dominating the park and facing down King Street to view her subjects. It is said that during the 1907 earthquake, the statue turned 180 degrees to face the hills, a sign some interpreted as a message that the city should expand northwards. The statue was later rotated, and in 1914, the garden was named Victoria Park in honor of the Queen. After Independence, the park was renamed in honor of St William Grant, the firebrand labor leader of the 1930s. The park still holds a sort of ceremonial appeal for Kingstonians, and once a year, the city's Christmas tree is lighted with much pomp and ceremony.

I am a Mecca for shoppers from all over the corporate area, and even many from out of town! Bargain hunters can find everything they need given the options. With the various arcades, the grand Coronation Market, the high street stores and the plethora of handcart and street vendors moving about, just about any wish can be granted, and any need fulfilled with the exchange of a few dollars. If you don't intend to buy and just want a sense of a Jamaican market, Coronation market is a necessary stop. It is crowded, noisy, chaotic and filled with countless delicious scents and amusing verbal advertisements and exchanges.

The Ward Theatre is Jamaica's largest and best-known performing arts theatre, and has a rich and fascinating history. That aside, the building itself is certainly worth a visit, but attending a performance there is clearly the best way to experience Jamaican theatre, history and culture firsthand. Call ahead or stop by the box office to see what's on. Usually the National Pantomime, an annual production of the Little Theatre Movement opens on December 26 and runs for a few months afterwards.

JAMAICAN TOWN/PLACE TRIVIA 16

I was once a former Spanish shipbuilding town, despite the fact that I was quite a distance inland! Over the years, I have prospered because of my proximity to the Bay, which is known for its wide fishing beach and bustling seaport. In the 1950s, Alumina Jamaica Limited renamed me Port Esquivel, an Anglicised version of the Spanish name. Today, the port still brings much needed bauxite earnings to me as Port Esquivel employs many of its residents.

In a country that has little regard for time, it is quite amazing that the clock standing in my centre Square, which was installed shortly after the English colonized Jamaica in the 17th century, still keeps perfect time! The iron clock tower is impressively well maintained and stands in the centre at the junction of two major roads.

A few kilometers north of me is Colbeck Castle, Jamaica's mystery building. Colbeck Castle was, for a long time, the largest building of its kind on the island. It is alleged that the castle was built by John Colbeck, a colonel of the British army that invaded Jamaica in 1655. Today the castle is in ruins, but its statuesque and imposing remains hint at the splendor it must have once been, surrounded by acres of pasture land with goats and cows occasionally sauntering by.

Even before one enters my town the smell of hot bread wafts across from Honeycrust Bakery, a landmark in the centre. Stop in for hot, fresh-baked hard dough breads, buns and pastries. If the breads are still in the oven, take a moment and ask inside for Mrs. Golding, the proprietor.

Mrs. Golding is usually around, and is a charming Jamaican lady who is quite involved in my social improvement.

JAMAICAN TOWN/PLACE TRIVIA 17

Today I'm a grown-up playground for mature free spirits. Yesterday I was the old seaside town, a favorite resort for the rich and famous who were attracted to the seclusion, sophistication and serenity and built elegant villas in the surrounding areas. I am one of the most accessible towns in Jamaica. Within my town, just about everywhere is within walking or bicycling distance. I am covered with graceful old buildings with Jamaican gingerbread verandas and elaborate fretwork transoms that evoke illusions of grandeur from a time when the banana trade was at its zenith, and movie stars mingled effortlessly with the local elite.

Visitors are encouraged to support local craft vendors. A short walk through my town is a most interesting and revealing trip. The Demontevin Lodge, the Court House, the ornate and amusing Village of St George shopping centre, and the old Fort George (now a popular High School). A short boat ride away is Navy Island, a tiny cay in the middle of the Harbor with a beautiful golden-sand beach and its own tropical rain forest. On the hill just behind my town are some sights worth seeing. The Parish Church with its brick entrance tower and tall arched windows is an impressive structure, while the vistas from the Bonnie View Hotel are sure to take your breath away. A few kilometers east are lavish villas, hotels and private homes of the village of San San are tucked sensuously away within lush emerald forests. Here the world-famous Frenchman's Cove Beach and San San Beach, together a once highly exclusive enclave of royalty and the very wealthy, are now open (for a small fee) to all connoisseurs of the idyllic life and tropical splendor.

Rafting on the Rio Grande is the ultimate vacation treat. The practice began in the early 20th century when flamboyant celebrity Errol Flynn noticed banana farmers from the interior highlands strapping the much valued fruits to bamboo rafts and floating them down the river to the wharf. Since then, privileged tourists have followed suit, becoming part of what is certainly one of the most magical experiences available anywhere in the world. The trip from the town of Berrydale in the hills to Rafter's Rest on the coast at times takes two and a half hours, a slow idyllic meander through rain forests and farmland on a thirty-foot raft steered expertly by a local "captain". Along the way, stop for a cool dip, enjoy a cold beverage or stop to chat with singing washerwomen and giggling children.

The Blue Lagoon, called "Blue Hole" by residents, is a small, almost landlocked cove, long reputed to be bottomless. Myriad shades of blue are surrounded by lush foliage, kept green by hundreds of tiny, underground mineral springs. The attraction is certainly one of the most scenic spots in Jamaica, as well as one of the most romantic places to enjoy a gourmet meal. Visitors are permitted to swim in the lagoon, and it is quite safe, despite the fanciful fables spun by locals about marine monsters lurking in its depths!

JAMAICAN TOWN/PLACE TRIVIA 18

I was considered to be the most cosmopolitan city in the western world, the "Paris of the Indies," I was a virtual goldmine. In the late 1700s, sugar was king and the profits from the sweet gold made the fortunes of men, families and nations. I had five newspapers, an active literary and fine arts society and–arguably my most distinctive attribute–fresh running water. I also housed a vast number of merchant shops, there were traders selling slaves, there was sugar, rum, fine furniture and logwood as well as the Albert George Market, the largest and most popular coastal market at the time. In the late 1800s, following the demise of sugar as a globally lucrative agricultural product, I steadily declined and the harbor, which once welcomed close to thirty ships in one day, saw less than that in a month. Now the sugar money is long gone, but many of the splendid original buildings remain, some in ruins, others masterfully restored to their former glory. In recognition of my rich historical legacy, I have been declared a World Heritage Site by the United Nations, and I am also a Jamaican National Monument.

I have maintained a long and distinguished reputation as a centre for commerce, both in the formal and informal sectors. Today my market is still one of the largest and most attended–especially on Wednesdays–when traders from all over the island congregate on the streets for "Bend-down market". On Wednesdays, consumers can purchase all sorts of foodstuff, haberdashery and home items at some of the best prices available on the north coast.

I have the largest collection of Georgian style buildings in the country. Some estimates, however, claim this collection is also the largest in the West Indies! A committee of professionals, academics and concerned citizens formed a Restoration Corporation, and this small group has been managing and overseeing the restoration of buildings. Perhaps the most encouraging trend in the restoration is the fact that not only are large public buildings and the grand stately homes of the merchant and planter classes are being restored, but also the small private homes of members of the working classes, the emancipated slaves and skilled artisans.

In order to capture my full essence a complete walking tour is recommended, there are some buildings that stand out, even more so after restoration. One such building is the Baptist Manse on Market Street near the waterfront, an imposing stone structure with a stately wooden staircase. Known to have housed the first Masonic Temple in Jamaica. Today it is a flagship structure in my restoration. The completed project will not only contribute to my physical renewal, but also to the cultural revival of the community. The lower level of the building will house a community-based initiative, while the upper level will be an art gallery displaying the work of local artists.

JAMAICAN TOWN/PLACE TRIVIA 19

I have a population of over 10,000 and growing. At night I change from a congested urban centre to a mellow yet lively scene of streets, lined with pan-chicken stalls and small pubs with patrons and Reggae music. My most interesting features are the twin salt ponds located just outside the town centre, which were once a key source of salt for the region. Several theories abound, but one of the most respected opinions is that during the earthquake of 1692, the land below what are now the ponds sank, leaving pockets of seawater almost completely enclosed by land. Due to evaporation, the water in the pond is extremely saline, at times recorded as being 15 times saltier than the seawater! A number of interesting and amusing stories abound as to the origin of the twin salt ponds. Some say the ponds were created after a dispute between two brothers in love with the same woman. According to that story, the older brother married the lady, but one afternoon when he travelled to Kingston on business, his wife and brother slept together, betraying his trust. Upon hearing of the dastardly deed, the older brother began to cry himself to death, and his tears fell into two salty puddles that drowned both the wife and the brother. Other stories tell of a dispute between the brothers, or some of a punishment for crimes the two brothers committed. So much for fables!

North of me lies the district of Heartsease, a sleepy little community that comes alive when Revival and Kumina meetings are held on the riverside near the old bridge. These meetings are loud and energetic, as believers in flowing garments and colorful head wraps sing and dance for hours at a time, moving to heavy, hypnotic drum rhythms. Also north lies Easington, which houses one of the most interesting geological formations in this part of the island–a sheer cliff that rises over one thousand feet high. Judgment Cliff, as it is called, is the most visible reminder of the 1692 earthquake that destroyed Port Royal. It was created by a landslide that happened when the earth moved. Many people were trapped beneath the heaps of dirt, including, it is said, a wicked slave owner who earned his fate. In 1955, the Jamaica National Trust erected a commemorative plaque in honor of National Hero Paul Bogle, leader of the Morant Bay Rebellion of 1865, who is associated with the area. Today, Easington is a sleepy community, with a bridge, road and civic square.

Another cozy spot is; 'Poor Man's Corner,' a well-known stop along the main highway; here you will find Bev's Restaurant, stop in and meet Bev, she has three frisky pet dogs at the side of her house, along with a beautiful collection of tropical birds under a sprawling cherry tree. Come by, have a bite to eat, play with the animals and take a few minutes to chat with Bev.

JAMAICAN TOWN/PLACE TRIVIA 20

Upon seizing control of Jamaica, the English invaders corrupted the "Boca d'agua" (water's mouth) of the Spanish road leading to me. The Rio Cobre runs through this valley, cutting a limestone gorge that is home to one of the most beautiful tropical watershed forests in the island. The road built along the course of the Rio Cobre is one of the oldest roadways in the island, and is both one of the most heavily trafficked and one of the most scenic routes to the north coast. From the road, towering cliffs and boulders seem to touch the sky at times, as the gorge is several hundred feet deep. I am located five miles north of the gorge and I am one of the oldest historic towns in Jamaica.

In my town you will find 'Flat Bridge,' literally a one-lane stone bridge that fords the massive and unpredictable Rio Cobre that has been the scene of what some may consider comical moments. Built in the 18th century to accommodate a trickle of non-motorized traffic, the bridge has not been modified since - even with the construction and paving of the new A1 highway. Not until the 1990s were traffic lights installed to regulate traffic; up till then, irate motorists would occasionally find themselves solidly squared off, facing an oncoming vehicle on the tiny bridge. With nowhere to turn around and neither side interested in reversing to allow the oncoming traffic to pass, motorists would sometimes be delayed for hours. This situation became so commonplace that it was immortalized in the 1973 Jamaican cult film, 'The Harder They Come.' Many have lost their lives at Flat Bridge and some have survived. Check out: 'My Miracle at Flat Bridge by George Peart.

The Gorge is an environmentalist's paradise. The Rio Cobre meanders through the moss-covered limestone cliffs and boulders, keeping the banks of the river emerald green, even in times of drought. The gorge is naturally well stocked with hundreds of species of tropical plants that at points seem to clothe the area completely, virtually unspoiled by human settlement.

JAMAICAN TOWN/PLACE TRIVIA 21

I am the longest village in Jamaica, laid out for more than five miles on either side of the South Coast highway and the Black River, both of which divide the community into East and West. Throughout the 18th century, Black River and me alternated as the capital of the parish of St Elizabeth. At one point in time, the river was the main transportation route for the parish, as road travel through the dense and humid mangrove swamps was treacherous at worst, miserable at best. My name was derived from the Spanish name for mahogany, when the main industry was the logging of mahogany trees, which were floated down the river to the wharf for export. Today the cashew nut has replaced mahogany lumber as the prime export of the area, and the Black River is no longer used to transport goods to the parish capital.

I was once home to one of the largest Jewish communities in Jamaica, and I am still of great importance to the existing Jamaican Jewish community today. There are many interesting remnants of that Jewish heritage, including an old graveyard with many telling tombstones. To date there is no formal site, but do contact the Jamaica National Heritage Trust for more information on Jewish settlements in Jamaica. The Jewish cemetery falls on the land of one Mr. Robinson, who respectfully maintains the tombs and is always accommodating to visitors.

I have cashews in abundance, but there is only one Cashoo. Cashews are grown all over the district, and cashew nuts are the area's largest cash crop. The only ostriches in Jamaica are bred at Cashoo Ostrich Park, a small attraction and working farm just outside the village. At Cashoo, there is horseback riding, river tubing and lots of prime picnic spots, with a restaurant and bar for grownups and a playground for children.

Beside the Texaco gas station along the main highway, two grey concrete tombs lie raised, almost in the middle of the road. One is unmarked, but the other belongs to one Thomas Jordan Spencer, said to be an ancestor to Winston Churchill and Diana Spencer. Why these men were buried here is a mystery, as are the circumstances surrounding their deaths – but just ask – almost anyone from the area is sure to give an animated account of their personal version of the story.

Mr. Robinson lives on the land right beside the cemetery. Mr. Robinson is a bit frail these days (he is rather elderly), but he will happily show you the tombstones that lie interspersed with his pineapple grounds.

JAMAICAN TOWN/PLACE TRIVIA 22

I am the home of Jamaica's famous Pickapeppa Sauce; a concoction of sweetness and spice, the thick brown condiment is a delightful addition to almost any Jamaican meal. The Pickapeppa Company Limited has been operating from its small factory since 1921, when the recipe was developed and first marketed among local gourmet connoisseurs.

Kirkvine Works, the first plant in Jamaica to actually process bauxite into aluminum, is still the largest plant on the island. At one point in the mid-20th century, Jamaica was the second largest exporter of bauxite/alumina in the world.

From my east is Blue Mountain Peak, which is only 60 miles away. It's an excellent view on a clear day. From the top of the hill you can view the tomb of the man who originally owned most of the land in the area, Alexander Woodburn Heron. Heron left instructions in his will to be buried there, and today the Windalco Bauxite Company maintains the tomb. Besides the tomb, it is an excellent lookout.

When you visit stop by the Pickapeppa factory for a tour (regular tours run from September to April), and ask for Joseph Lyn Kee Chow, oldest member of the Lyn Kee Chow family, the founders of the company. He may not be around, since he is semi-retired, but he may turn up while you are there. He does that occasionally, just to make sure that all is going well!

JAMAICAN TOWN/PLACE TRIVIA 23

I was originally called Santa Gloria by Christopher Columbus and was once the capital of the similarly named "Garden Parish", home to the island's first city, and birthplace of Marcus Mosiah Garvey–Jamaican National Hero and pioneer in Black Nationalism and Pan-Africanism. I display many old historic buildings and monuments set between the brilliant green mountains and the royal blue Caribbean Sea. The historic courthouse (built in 1860) and fort (built in 1750) have both witnessed many years of hardship, conflict and brutality and now stand as testimony to the understated strength and character of this town. Also of note are the statues of Marcus Garvey and Christopher Columbus, each standing at opposite ends. As parish capital, I attract visitors from all over the mostly rural inland areas. As a result, I look and feels like ol' time Jamaica, where the entire town, even the small side lanes, radiates a cosmopolitan blend of people-on-official-business, people-on-personal-business and people with not much else to do but socialize, all dressed accordingly.

Local legend maintains that there is a flammable body of water near the Police Station. Apparently, this spring can be lit and burn continuously until extinguished by waters from the same spring. The elusive spring is also said to have remarkable healing properties for those who find it. Please note: this story may be at best wild conjecture, but investigating its validity may offer the opportunity to make new friends!

Marcus Garvey, the charismatic and influential black activist and organizer spent his youth here before moving to Kingston, where he started his political life. His messages of black solidarity and self-determination paved the way for many black Pan-Africanist leaders around the world, while in Jamaica his messages defined the philosophy of the Rastafari movement. A son of a well-respected local citizen, Garvey embodied the spirit of the Jamaican working classes and eloquently represented the interests of people from the entire African Diaspora by organizing the United Negro Improvement Association (UNIA), a Black Nationalist movement that in its prime had over one million supporters worldwide.

A walking tour around my town is easy and well worth the effort. Start on either side, but as you make your way across, do take note of the Parish Library, Garvey's Market Street house, the Courthouse, the old Fort, the Baptist Church on Main Street, Our Lady of Perpetual Help Catholic Church, the market and the Columbus statue my west side. I am compact and easy to get around, so a visit here can be done on the same day as the Seville/Maima Heritage tour. It is almost inevitable that tour of my town will end near to or at the beach, a delightful end to an intriguing journey through Jamaica's heritage.

JAMAICAN TOWN/PLACE TRIVIA 24

I am one of the oldest continuously settled areas in Jamaica, yet, I have been one of the most sparsely populated places on the island. I receive very little of the rainfall that keeps most of Jamaica green and lush, and only a small fraction of the less than 30-inches per year is retained in the highly porous limestone soil. The result is an extremely arid area with many rare species of flora and fauna specifically adapted to the environment. Ecologically rich as I am with no continuous fresh water supply, human communities have traditionally been small and transient. I was originally settled by the island's first inhabitants, the Tainos, then later by groups of runaway slaves and communities of hunters and fishers determined to withstand the region's harsh terrain. Today there are plans to turn me into a reserve for the protection of the important natural resources and the unique habitats of endangered and protected species of flora and fauna.

I have become one of the most popular bathing beaches on the South Coast because of the spirit of community and the generally mellow vibe of the beach. Spend a day with me and you will see fishing boats coming ashore intermittently, intercepted on the beach by hagglers who either cook on the beach or take the fish to be sold inland.

The fishmongers on the beach first created "festival", a sort of sweet bread usually served with fish, or so they claim. The seemingly simple recipe is often imitated, but rarely duplicated successfully. Kingstonians have many theories about this–some claim that a sprinkling of sand is the secret ingredient; others claim that a dash of seawater mixed into the batter is the trick. Either way, it is a tasty and filling complement to a meal of fresh escoviched fish that is a staple on the beach. Miss May, operates one of the most popular spots to enjoy a meal. Miss May is one of the longest-standing cooks, and her shack, occasionally run by one of her children, is easy to find from the road. Like many of the other vendors on the beach, Miss May specializes in fish and festival, although she will quickly identify someone to prepare lobster on request. The beauty is, just about anything is possible, so if one vendor's prices or location doesn't suit you, there are close to 100 vendors on the beach to choose from.

I am surrounded by hills that carry my name and I am one of the last remaining habitats of the iguana, a large reptile that once roamed the entire island. Take a short hike to meet one of these colorful and stately creatures, but do not attempt to catch or even touch one–the iguana is a protected species under Jamaican law.

JAMAICAN TOWN/PLACE TRIVIA 25

I am one of Jamaica's national treasures. Globally, it is as well known as Reggae and equally stimulating. There are few places where the Arawak name "Xayamaca"–land of rivers and springs - is more apt. The Spaniards called me "Las Chorreras"–the waterfalls or springs–and I am truly one of the most beautiful spots on the island. A stone's throw from Ocho Rios, one of Jamaica's fastest growing resort centers, I am unique!

I am described as a living and growing phenomenon, I continuously regenerate myself from deposits of travertine rock, the result of precipitation of calcium carbonate from the river, as it flows over the falls. The small dome-shaped cataracts are usually associated with thermal spring activity found in limestone caves. This, combined with its location near to the sea, gives me the distinction of being the only one of its kind in the Caribbean, if not the world.

I bring laughter to both young and old and when you leave me, you leave with a sense of youthfulness and pride.

JAMAICAN TOWN/PLACE TRIVIA 26

I am approximately 20 kilometers north of Kingston and I am known for my most famous attribute, a Botanical Garden. I was established in 1862 to facilitate the relocation of the Bath Botanical Gardens, making me one of the oldest public botanical gardens in the western hemisphere. I am the most richly stocked in the Caribbean, boasting over 180 species of palm and at least 400 specimens of other flora. The land I occupy is in the cool, verdant hills of St Mary. It is divided by the main road to Junction with another end adjacent to a rocky river bed where women from the village can sometimes be seen washing clothes in the small seasonal stream. Many of the trees and plants introduced to Jamaica were first planted here, most notably the Bombay mango, navel orange and tangerine. Other important exotic trees, palms and shrubs include: Cestrum Nocturnum (Night Jasmine), Spathodea Campanulata (Flame of the Forest), Litchi Chinensis (Chinese Guinep) and Sanchezia Nobilis (Hummingbird Fountain). All 15 acres are open to the public, and is a popular picnic spot for Kingstonians eager for a break from the city. The Wag Water River flows through me parallel to the botanical gardens, adding to the serenity and pristine beauty of the area.

I am the ideal location for a day's outing and picnics. Be sure to stop to look at the more than 25 varieties of palm trees, some of which are over 100 years old!

Unsung Heroes

R HENRY LOWE

Dr. Henry Lowe is a Jamaican scientist involved in developing Jamaican plants like the Ball Moss as the treatment for cancer.

He was educated at Manchester University, England where he gained the Ph.D. in Medicinal Chemistry.

His career experience includes head of the science department at the former College of Arts, Science and Technology (CAST), executive chairman of Blue Cross of Jamaica, and is currently the founding chairman of the Environment Health Foundation at the Bio-Tech R&D Institute in Jamaica. In October 2008, following intense research he discovered and announced to the world the healing benefits of Ball Moss in treating forms of cancers, particularly prostate cancer. He made a presentation of his research findings to the world scientific community at Ehrlich II, the 2nd World Conference on Magic Bullets in Nurnberg, Germany. The response was overwhelming.

He and his fellow scientists are involved in continuing research at the Bio-Tech R&D Institute with the primary mission of developing biological materials, especially those of local origins, for wealth creation.

His vision is for the Institute is to act as a catalyst for the development of biotechnology as a business in Jamaica.

PROF. G. LALOR, 1930:

A physical chemist Prof. Lalor is known for the discovery of haematoxylin, a substance extracted from logwood and used in the diagnosis of cancer. Now retired from UWI, he served as a lecturer, creator of UWIDITE, the system of distance learning, and of Jamaica's first geo-chemical map, which uncovered many previously unidentified elements. 1974-1995: He was the Pro-Vice Chancellor of UWI 1991: Became the second principal of the Mona campus. He remains involved in various research projects.

PROF. LOUIS GRANT, M.D., C.H., M.P.H., DIP BACT., FAPHA, F.C. PATH, F.A.A.N. (1913-1993)

A microbiologist and pathologist, Prof. Louis Grant was affiliated with the University of the West Indies for 20 years where he achieved the highest academic honour, being named professor emeritus in microbiology. Young Louis Grant was surrounded by science from an early age. Born in Vere, Clarendon in 1913, his father worked in a chemical laboratory at the Appleton Estate. As a student, Grant showed promise and received the Vere Trust scholarship to attend Jamaica College. He went on to Edinburgh University in Scotland and later specialised in tropical microbiology at the London School of Tropical Medicine and Hygiene. Prof. Grant then returned to Jamaica serving his country as a medical doctor, microbiologist and pathologist.

Tubercolosis: In the 1940s Dr. Grant dreamed of a Jamaica with less disease and he decided to focus on tuberculosis, a disease then plaguing the island. He asked the World Health Organisation (WHO) and UNICEF for a grant to begin an inoculation campaign amongst Jamaican children. Joined by Dr. Ronald Lampart, Dr. Grant completed a mass vaccination that is credited with helping to break the cycle of infection and halt the spread of the dreaded disease.

CURDELL BRIDGE

Curdell Bridge turned 97 on July 29, 2012 and she models health, wellness and youth. She lives by Dr. Vendryes's four pillars but she has a fifth pillar; 'The power of the word.' She is one of the most positive Jamaican's you will ever meet, always looking on the brighter side of life. She was never held back by her circumstances. Started life on dirt floor with her husband, had 12 children, six alive today, four of which are doctors and she sees age as just a number. She lives alone, manages her farm, pays her taxes and still travels occasionally to the States. She wakes up each day with an attitude of gratitude thanking God for the gift of life. Curdell is young, vibrant, positive and God-fearing. She is rich in spirit and we could all take a page from her book. Her advice: "Invest in your children and I promise it will pay big dividends and remember life and death is in the power of the tongue, speak life!"

ELGETA THOMPSON MARTIN: President/Caribbean Music Festival

"MOVER & SHAKER." A permanent fixture within the South Florida community, Elgeta and her hardworking Caribbean Music Festival committee and Clint O'Neil Needy Kids of Jamaica, Inc work tirelessly to address the needs of children in Jamaica, South Florida and other Caribbean islands, though she only has one biological child she mothers thousands through her commitment to underprivileged children.

For the past 29 years Elgeta has been responsible for organizing one of the most successful black tie events held in South Florida to celebrate Jamaica's Independence on the last Saturday of July, year after year. If you have never attended one of these events you owe it to yourself to come celebrate Jamaica's Independence and experience the difference.

Elgeta is a giver, a woman of strength and courage! Her two grand children are her cherished treasures.

SANDY ISAACS, Owner/CEO of Breakaway Moments

If you have ever attended a 'Jamaican Event' in Orlando, chances are Sandy Isaacs had something to do with it! Sandy has been active in her local community as the leader of the 'Confidence In Crisis' Women's Group which she started with the help of her church. She was the Coordinator of a Mission Trip to benefit Arthur Wint Basic School in Lucea, Hanover in 2007. Sandy is always contacting her fellow Jamaicans to seek help for Jamaicans in crisis whether in Jamaica or any part of the world. She does this with passion and a resolve that she must get the help she's seeking because there is a dire need. If Sandy Isaacs ever reaches out to you, please take a moment to respond, chances are it's a 911 call to help a fellow Jamaican. Sandy is the recipient of numerous recognition, leadership and community service awards. She is the mother of five wonderful children.

JODY-ANNE MAXWELL

Scripps National Spelling Bee Competition 1998: A new hero emerged from Jamaica in May 1998, and to this day she still remains a hero. A 12-year-old girl from Kingston with a winsome smile and steely determination whose David vs. Goliath victory at the National Spelling Bee has enthralled Jamaicans both on the island and in the large immigrant communities such as New York City and Florida.

Jody-Anne Maxwell, with precise diction flavored by her lilting accent, spelled "chiaroscurist" before a packed hall in Washington on Thursday, becoming the Bee's first foreign champion in its 71 years. She defeated 248 other finalists, including a handful from the Bahamas and Mexico, the only other foreign nations represented.

GIFTON WRIGHT

Fourteen year old Gifton Wright of Spanish Town placed 4th in the Scripps National Spelling Bee Competition, 2012. Gifton likes participating in competitions, and he enjoys singing and dancing. In his spare time he participates in track and field and football, and he plays checkers and computer games. At school (Ardenne High School) , Gifton is deputy head boy. He is also on the Quiz team, and participates in the chess and math clubs. He excels in math and earned the highest math grade in his school. Gifton is learning to speak French and hopes to become a doctor someday.

BUNNY GRANT

Welterweight boxer: Bunny Grant brought early attention to Jamaican sports as the first Jamaican to fight for a world boxing title when he fought the American champion Eddie Perkins or the World Junior Welterweight title in 1964. Unfortunately he lost the bout on points. Before this, on August 5, 1962, independence eve, he won the Commonwealth lightweight title beating Britain's Dave Charnley. He was also the Latin American Junior Welterweight champion. In his 15 year career he fought eight world champions in the lightweight and welterweight divisions and had a professional record of 102 fights, 86 wins, 10 losses and six draws. In 1965, Ring Magazine named Bunny as the number one contender for Carlos Ortiz's world title, and between 1963 and 1968, he was ranked in the top 10 in the junior welterweight division.

SPENCE BOTHERS, MEL AND MAL

Track and Field: Spence bothers, Mel and Mal, born January 2, 1936. The brothers were always serious contenders winning several medals in the Pan-American Games. Mel was a silver medalist in the 1955 Pan American Games and he was also a part of the winning team in Central America at the Caribbean Games held in 1962. Mel had a best time of 46.94. In 1960 Mal ran in the 4 x 100 relay in Rome, Italy and was awarded a bronze medal, his best time was 46.4. They competed between 1955-1964.

ARTHUR "DUKE REID"

Arthur "Duke Reid" record producer and DJ must be mentioned. He popularized the sound system that blared hits at Jamaican dances in the 1960s. He founded The Trojan sound system that drew large crowds at the 'sessions" he played at in Kingston; and recorded Jamaican ska and rock steady artists on his Treasure Isle record label. He made artists like Justin Hinds and the Dominoes, and DJ 'toaster' U-Roy popular.

COUNT PRINCE MILLER

Count Prince Miller was a Jamaican entertainer who made his song *Mule Train* extremely popular in the 1960s. He also acted in several films winning the Best Male Actor Award at the 2006 Black Film Makers' International Awards Ceremony, in London, England.

CARLOS MALCOLM

Carlos Malcolm (Band Leader and Composer) When the conversation turns to Jamaican popular bands, Byron Lee and the Dragonaires is often mentioned. But during the 60s another band led by professional musician Carlos Malcolm gave Byron Lee strong competition. Malcolm formed the Afro-Jamaican Rythms in 1963, and the band which featured a heavy brass section (playing a blend of ska, mento and jazz), drew crowds of dancers wherever it played, mainly at the former Sombrero Club on Molynes Road. Malcolm who composed most of the band's hits like *Rukumbine* and *Bonanza* was also a talented trombonist and percussionist. He delighted in composing and performing Ska music, and was once called the Quincy Jones of Ska.

One of his impressive achievements was to be appointed director of the "island content" of the musical score of the James Bond film *Dr. No* filmed in Jamaica.

DERRICK HARRIOTT

Derrick Harriott was another pioneer in Jamaican music. The singer had numerous hits, including, *The Loser, Walk the Streets at Night, Do I worry* and *Solomon, Born to Love You* during the 60's and 70s and his recordings were "must plays" at dances and parties in Jamaica and its Diaspora. Harriott also ran the successful "One Stop" record shops in down town Kingston and up-town.

SONIA POTTINGER

Sonia Pottinger (Miss P) was Jamaica's first female record producer, producing hits for several artists at her Tip-Top studios from the mid 1960s. After producing the hit "Every Night" by Joe White and Chuck, she produced records for Ken Boothe, Alton Ellis and Toots & the Maytals on the Tip Top, Gay Feet and Rainbow labels. She bought the Treasure Isle label from Duke Reid in 1974 when he fell ill, and contested and won the rights to the vast Treasure Isle catalog in 2009, a year before she passed.

JACKIE MITTOO

Jackie Mittoo was one of Jamaica's best pianist and organist. He became popular as the piano and keyboard player for the iconic Skatalites band in the 1960s, and was the keyboard player, composer arranger and producer for Studio One owned by Coxsone Dodd. His keyboard artistry can be heard on recordings by Bob Marley and the Wailers, Jimmy Cliff, the Heptones, Delroy Wilson and Alton Ellis.

KENNETH KHOURI

Kenneth Khouri, founder, owner of Federal Records in Kingston was another top Jamaican record producer, One of Khouri's earlier associate was former Jamaican PM and JLP leader, Edward Seaga, who owned the franchise for Colombia Records in Jamaica. When Seaga focused on politics, Khouri sold Seaga's business to Byron Lee, and that business became the popular Dynamic Sounds.

Khouri recorded many artists, and had a strong influence on contemporary producers like Coxsone Dodd and Duke Reid. When he retired he sold Federal Records to Bob Marley, and it became Tuff Gong International.

U-ROY

U-Roy (Ewart Beckford) was one of Jamaica's earliest DJ's, or toasters, as they were called back in the 60s and 70s. These toasters had the talent for talking, usually in rhyme over the lyrics and music of other artist's recordings.

Although U Roy was toasting before 1970, in that year he was 'discovered' by singer John Holt, who heard him toasting one of Holt's records and became involved in his career. U-Roy went on to record over other artists recordings for Duke Reid, and released big hits like *Wake the Town*, *Rule the Nation* and *Wear You to the Ball.* He started a trend that quickly developed and DJ's, later rap artists, developed across Jamaica and internationally. The Jamaicans DJs influenced by U Roy, includes Big Youth, Scotty, and Dennis Alcapone.

MORE NATION BUILDERS

Fifty years span many lifetimes, and the space allotted to journalists provides limitations to honor the hundreds of Jamaicans that played some role in building our nation, and who either received scant commendation, or may have been forgotten over the passage of time. However, it would be remiss not to briefly mention the following dedicated Jamaicans in the areas of :

FINANCE: Bank of Jamaica governors, G. Arthur Brown and Headley Brown, Don Banks, Director, National Commercial Bank, Basil Buck, Jamaica Stock Exchange, Douglas Folks, Mutual Security Bank, Dr. Marshall Hall (Public economics), Pamela Watson, CPA.

JOURNALISM

Morris Cargill, John Maxwell, Theodore Sealy, Uriel Salmon, Archie Lindo, Barbara Gloudon, Barbara Ellington. Hazelle Rogers, Member of the Florida House of Representatives.

THE LABOR MOVEMENT

Carlyle Dunkley (NWU), Hopeton Caven (TUC), Lascelles Beckford (BITU).

PUBLIC SERVICE: Corrine McClarty–Jampro, Winnie Risden Hunter–Jamaica Information Service, Joyce Robinson–Jamaica Library Services and the HEART Foundation, Clover Thompson–Jamaica Cultural Development Commission (and service to education as principal of the Denham Town Comprehensive High School, Allan Kirton (Permanent Secretary Prime Minister's Office), Carole Guntley–Tourism, Godfrey Dyer–Tourism, Horace Barber–Financial Secretary and Governor–BOJ,, Ken Smith and Ira Rowe (Chief Justices).

RELIGION

Rev. Herman Spence and Rev. Don Taylor (Anglicans), Bishop U.S. Hastings (Moravian), Rev. Oliver Daley (United Church), Rev. Horace D. Ward, Rev. Cyril Evans Bailey Methodist).

BROADCASTING

Uriel Alridge, Fae Ellington, Barry Gordon (Barry G.), Allan Magnus, Desmond Chambers, Roy Reid, Dorothy Lacroix (Dotty Dean), Marie Garth, Neville Willoughby, Winsome Charlton (Lady C.), Don Daley, Eddie Edwards, John T, Denver Silvera.

MEDICINE:

Dr. Sam Street–Surgeon, Dr. Don Christian–Cardiologist, Dr. Alfred Lockhart–Ophthalmologist, Dr. Harold Johnson–Medical Officer of Health, Professor Dr.Louis Grant–Microbiologist and pathologist.

COMMUNITY BUILDERS

Hazelle Rogers was born in Jamaica on September 28, 1952. She received early education in Jamaica, up to high school and later migrated to New York in 1969 before settling in Lauderdale Lakes, Florida. She earned a Bachelor of Science degree in management from University of Phoenix in 2003.

Hazelle is a member of the Democratic Party and was the first Jamaican elected official on the Lauderdale Lakes City Commission. In 2008 she became the first person of Jamaican descent to be elected to the Florida House of Representative, and continues to serve in that House.

She was also co-chair of the United Negro College Fund that plays a significant role in the higher education of Black youth. Outside of representational politics her career is in real estate. Her hobbies are dancing, netball and walking. She is married to Clifton Rogers.

Dale Holness, Broward County Commissioner District 9, "A Man Of Action." Commissioner Holness took the initiative to introduce KAPOW (Kids And the Power Of Work) to two Broward Elementary Schools, focused on Education!

He founded the Chamber of Commerce in the City of Lauderhill. Under his patronage the chamber's membership now includes over 200 businesses. Serious about the growth of businesses in the community!

Commissioner Holness persuaded the city to agree to grant seniors an addition $2500 in homestead exemption to lower their property taxes. Passionate about our Seniors!

Aston Lue is founder of Ocho Rios-Miami, which provides specialty foods serving the Jamaican, Caribbean and Hispanic market. He traces his strong work ethic to both sets of his roots and considers himself a Chinese Jamaican American.

Aston Lue is no doubt a 'Community Builder' and is known for his generosity. Aston and his wife Michelle are avid supporters for most Caribbean events, displaying products and giving attendees an opportunity to sample the 'Ocho Rios' brand. Tons of folks will leave these events with complementary products. While Aston is out exhibiting his philanthropic spirit, Leroy Tenn, the General Manager for the company is back in the office ensuring the success of the corporation.

ORGANIZATIONS/CORPORATIONS:

WAVS 1170 AM, Jamaica Awareness, Caribbean Heart Menders, It Takes A Village, Anthony Baker Institute (ABI), Jamaica Gleaner, Jamaica Observer, National Weekly, Caribbean Today, Caribbean-American Commentary Newspaper, Caribbean Voice, CRI Communications, Douglas Chiropractic, Goldson Spine Rehabilitation, A Place of Restoration, Housing Foundation of America,Sunshine Production Enterprises, Island TV, Nelrak Child Development

Center, Caribbean American Chamber of Commerce, Future Movement Radio, South Florida Caribbean News, Mandell Chiropractic Centre, Princess PM Productions, Jamaica United Relief Association, The Big Blue and You.

MORE FACTS ON JAMAICAN BEAUTY/FASHION

Beauty Related: Debbie Campbell placed third in 1979, as did Sandra Campbell in 1981; Allison Barnett fifth in 1985, Erica Aquart sixth in 1990. Sandra Foster fourth in 1991(she later placed in the top 10 in Miss Universe) and Christine Straw, sixth in 1998.

Other prominent Jamaican beauty queens included Mitzie Constantine (later Seaga), Laurel Williams, Karlene Waddell, and Joan McDonald (famous as Jamaica's truly African-Jamaican beauty).

Mickey Haughton-James of Spartan Health Club played a significant role in producing the Miss Jamaican World beauty pageant in the 1970s and 80s. Many Jamaican beauties and female winners of body-building competitions were trained at the Spartan Gym.

Kingsley Cooper also played a role in the development of beauty pageants and fashion in Jamaica through his company Pulse Investments Ltd., and as producer of the Miss Universe Jamaica pageant.

Did You Know?

All information in this segment provided by the Jamaica Tourist Board

Jamaica's First Newspaper: The weekly Jamaica Courant was our first newspaper. The first printing press was started in 1718 and the 1st issue was printed on 28 May 1718 by R. Baldwin and sold for one bit which was then worth seven pence half-penny.

Fact on Jamaica Tourist Board: The JTB was established on April 1, 1955

Falmouth families: At one time the entire coasted area between Falmouth and Montego Bay was owned by two families - "The Barretts took from Little River to Falmouth, the Lawrences from Little River to Montego Bay". The first Barretts came to Jamaica with the English army of conquest in 1655 and obtained extensive land grants in the area. Lawrence descendants at one time owned estates which included Ironshore, Running Gut (Half Moon estate) and Fairfield.

Fort Charles: Fort Charles at Port Royal named after Charles II was built during his reign and both sides of the fort were washed by the sea while the inland side forms what is the Parade Ground today. Fort Charles became the headquarters of the Royal Navy in the 18th century and carried a full complement of 104 guns and never once attacked in its history.

Splendid houses built on a bet: Four wealthy Kingston merchants once took a bet to see who could build the most splendid town residence, only to secure affections from Teresia Constantia. Only one of the houses survived, Headquarters House on Duke Street built by Thomas Hibbert in the 1750's and known originally as Hibbert House. The other houses were Constantine House on Higholborn Street and Bull and Harmony Hall on Hanover Street.

Cinchona: The medicine quinine is taken from the cinchona tree grown in Jamaica. The value of quinine in the treatment of malaria fever was known to the Indians of Peru and other American countries from earlier times. It was noticed by the Europeans in 1638 when it cured the Countess Cinchon. The plant was then named in her honor.

First Coconut tree in Jamaica: A stone monument on the Palisadoes near to Port Royal records that "the first coconut tree was planted March 4, 1869 by John Norton Esquire Superintendent of the General Penitentiary". Within 20 years 20,000 trees had been planted and flourished for a while, an ambitious project aimed at covering the Palisadoes in Coconut trees. Eventually disease destroyed them leaving only the stone monument.

Getting High On Water: Around the 18th century fashionable young men in Jamaica discovered a novel method of intoxication–water! This was medicinal water which flows the mineral springs at Bathe, St. Thomas. Historian Edward Long noted that taking the first drink diffuses a thrilling glow over the body, and continued use enlivens the spirits.

The Abeng: The Abeng made from a cow horn known as the Akete was the main instrument of communication among the Maroons during the wars. They had a regular series of calls on the horn which summoned each other over great distances, such as warnings of the soldiers approaching. Even today horn-men still blow the Abeng.

Poor Cricket Club: David Ellington a poor hackney carriage drive founded the Lucas Cricket Club in Kingston and funded it out of his own pocket. It was named after the first Englishman to bring a cricket team to Jamaica (1895), known as Slade Lucas. He produced two of the finest batsmen of this century–J.K. Holt Snr. and George Headley.

Ortanique: The Ortanique is unique to Jamaica and is a cross between a Tangerine and an Orange. Its common name is derived from the words orange, tangerine and unique.

National Heritage: The Worthy Park Sugar Estate, almost in the middle of the island, was founded in 1670 by Francis Price. It is the oldest sugar estate in continuous production.

Public notice needed to travel: It was not easy to leave Jamaica in the early days not only because transportation was slow but because the law required that no one could leave the island without first publicly advertising his intentions three weeks in advance. This was mainly to protect creditors from people even captains of ships who refused to pay and then skipped the country.

Shark Papers: In 1799 when Britain was at war with France a ship called *The Nancy* was seized by the British and taken to Port Royal for unlawful trading. The Captain swore that his vessel was American, but then another British ship arrived and produced documents found inside a shark showing that the captain was lying. The papers can be seen at the Institute of Jamaica.

Old Woman Savanna: In Clarendon, running roughly from Kellits to Crofts Hill there is an area known as Old Woman's Savanna. It appeared so on earliest maps and apparently the old woman was a Spaniard who refused to leave Jamaica when the English captured the island in 1655, even though her house and property in Spanish Town were seized. She received permission to retire to her hato in the country thus giving the name to the area.

Christians and Jews unite: Myer Lyon (Leoni) came to Jamaica in 1789 and became the finest cantor in the synagogue then located at the corner of Barry and Orange Streets in Kingston. He adapted the Slavic melody to the ancient Hebrew Hymn text *Yigdal* which is a standard in most Ashkenazi synagogues. He wrote the hymn *The God of Abraham Praise* which became a standard in many Christian churches. He is buried in the old Jewish cemetery on Elletson Road near Windward Road in Kingston.

Blackbeard: Edward Teach, the notorious pirate known as Blackbeard was born in Spanish Town 'of very creditable parents.' He went to sea at age 15 and drifted into piracy. By the turn of the 18th century he was in command of his own vessel. Blackbeard was so called because he had a beard so huge that he twisted it into tails and tied it with ribbons. Adding to his ferocious appearance, he also stick fuses under his hat and light them as he battle. It was said that he is supposed to have had 14 wives.

National Heritage: The Worthy Park Sugar Estate, almost in the middle of the island, was founded in 1670 by Francis Price. It is the oldest sugar estate in continuous production.

Salt from Hellshire: The Great Salt Pond in the Hellshire Hills, St. Catherine was extensively mined for salt and there were two salt works at Salt Pond Hill operated by Capt. Joseph Noye in the 18th century, and in one year he produced 10,000 bushels of salts. In 1670 an agreement was made with St. Thomas Modyford who patented adjoining lands of St. Thomas in the Vale and St. Dorothy to supply them with salt at a low rate.

University Chapel: The University Chapel at the University of the West Indies was originally a sugar warehouse? The warehouse was once a part of Gales Valley Estate in Trelawny. The building was dismantled stone by stone and removed to Mona where it was rebuilt exactly as it was at the estate.

Kingston Harbour: Kingston is built around the 7th largest natural harbour in the world? She is also home to other natural attractions including the Royal Botanical Gardens at Hope and Cinchona Gardens.

Postage Stamps: British stamps were first used in the colonies of Jamaica on May 8, 1858. Jamaica gained its own stamps in 1860 with values having different colours from one six-pence and one shilling which bore the head of Queen Victoria, the reigning monarch. There was also the introduction of the half-penny stamp (stamp cut diagonally). The first pictorial stamp was in1900, unpopular at first, then reissued in black and red the next year.

First Mango Plant: The first mango plants introduced into Jamaica were 'captured' on the high seas on their way from the East Indians to the West Indies by Lord Rodney's ship H.M.S Flora in 1782. They were first planted at the private garden at Gordon Town, St. Andrew, belonging to Hinton East. The seedlings were numbered on arrival, eg. The number eleven. The Bombay mango was introduced later in 1868 at Castleton Gardens.

Plantain Garden River: The Plantain Garden River in St Thomas is the only river in Jamaica that flows to the east.

Duppy Fly Trap: Duppy Fly Trap is the local name of a plant (Aristolochia Grandiaflora) which is an insect-trapping flower. The plant does not eat the insect but use it as a means of propagation. The plant gives off an unpleasant odor which attracts flies and small insects. After being trapped inside the flower and fully covered with pollen grains, they are allowed to escape, so that when attracted into another "Duppy Fly Trap", the powder is rubbed off and fertilization takes place.

Memories of "Dem Good Old Days,

Fudgie: The man pushing his colorful cart selling icecicles and ice cream on a little stick–called fudge–on hot summer days.

Peanut man: The peanut man, pushing his cart, upon which is affixed a whistle–selling peanuts in little brown paper or cone shaped bags.

Sail Boats: Children racing "boats" made of fudge sticks in the flowing street gutters after a heavy rain-shower.

Teenage Dance Party: The popular program for teens on JBC radio, hosted by Sonny Bradshaw. Teens across the island would tune in to this program.

Other popular announcers back then...

Charlie Babcock (The Cool Fool), Tony Verity, Roy Reid, Radcliffe Butler

Alan Magnus has been literally waking up Jamaica for over 40 years now joined by the phenomenal Paula- Anne Porter, what a team!

Skateland–at Rainbow Club in Half Way Tree, (HWT), where the youth roller skated to R&B music. Most teens living in the city would experience this energetic and competitive sport.

Night Clubs like ***Glass Bucket*** in HWT and ***Sombrero*** on Molynes Road where the young would dance ska, reggae, rock-steady, etc. to bands like Carlos Malcolm and the Troubadours, The Vikings, Tomorrows Children and Byron Lee and the Dragonaires. Some teens would sneak away with their boyfriends and go 'rent a tile' for the night. And later end up at ***Speedy Jerk Shop*** (the best jerk pork then), on Molynes Road.

Walking without fear with your girlfriend on moonlight nights anywhere in Kingston, and going to ***Dairy Products*** on HWT Road for slim-jims and hamburger.

And would often times end up at ***Carib Theatre*** in Cross Roads for Saturday evening matinees. Yeah, these were the uptown teens, getting a taste of courting...

And by the way for our house parties back then, everyone carried music, food or drinks. So we were doing 'Pot Luck' way before we came to America.

Sometimes we would pile up in the green and silver Jolly Joseph (JOS) bus and ride to ***Red-Gal-Ring*** club in Red Hills to dance to the beat of Merritones Disco, which is still going strong today. Shout out to Winston Blake and the rest of the crew!

By the way our shopping was not done at Burdines and Macys, most of our shopping was done at; ***Nathans, Times Store, London Shop*** and ***Issas*** on King Street in Kingston. When the guys stepped out in their 3 piece suit and ting, the girls were in their halter-top, so much so they almost gave the guys a heart attack... They were seriously too hot to trot!

Walking with lots of friends on a dark early morning from a fete at the UWI Student Union because all the buses had stopped running and we had no money to take a cab. And you think we'd be upset? NO! We took the opportunity to have more fun, walking and talking and enjoying the fresh morning wind gently brushing across our faces. Wow what Freedom!

Did you ever meet **Sir Alexander Bustamante** and **Norman Manley** our National Heroes? They were cousins. Well some of us did. What noble men? May their souls R.I.P.

Participating in a protest rally with prime minister to be, **Michael Manley,** during the historic JBC strike aftermath and getting hit with a police baton for lying in King Street with Michael. My good friend really experienced this and it made him a more committed comrade up to this day.

Rising from your seat and standing to attention each time the Jamaican National anthem is played. Let truth be told, many of us do this for the American anthem but do we always do this when the Jamaican anthem is played?

Listening to a little sound box called **Rediffusion,** operated by Radio Jamaica and only able to get one station. I honestly remember a big brown and beige radio my father had and he would take it to the shop in the mornings and bring it back home at nights. So if we wanted to listen to **"Dulcimina,"** we had to go to the shop, sit on the bench and listen.

Watching the only black and white JBC channel on Jamaican TV. This one here is referring to Kingstonians, many country folk did not see TV until they were 10 or older.

Most country folk did not have running water they had to catch water from the spring, and bring it home with a cotta on the head to cushion the weight of the pail. It was limited but it had to stretch.

How about when water was scarce, Mama and Daddy would tidy in the basin first then the children would tidy in the same water and everyone went to sleep believing that they were clean.

So when the Kingston folks go to the theatres and the ice cream parlors the country folks go to church instead, in most cases 3-6 times a week. That's why when most of them backslide they find their way back home, just like the prodigal son.

The popular public **Gun-Boat Beach** and beach picnics on the Palisadoes Road is where the people from Kingston would frequent. But the only time the people from country would see Gun-Boat beach is when they would be driving a farm worker to the airport who was going to America.

Do you remember when our dollar was stronger than the US dollar? Well in 2012 it was $90.00JA to $1.00US. Dear God, what will it be in 10 years. Reflect for a moment on Pound, Shillings and Pence. One shilling could buy a cocoa-bread and patty and today $1.00 cannot even buy an icy mint.

So the upper and middle class families would participate in Motor car races at **Vernam Field** in May Pen, Clarendon or Cross country motor car rallies sponsored by Shell and Texaco. That was then and this is now, though many things have changed about Jamaica, I believe classism still exists to some extent.

Therefore, I encourage every Jamaican who quietly faces this dilemma, to rise above classism, embrace your difference, whether you are from the city or the country, it doesn't matter, rich or poor doesn't make a difference. Let us model our 'Trendsetters' and embrace national pride in becoming an agent of change and help make a positive difference as a Jamaican, wherever we are in the world. Let us adopt the words of Bob Marley's *Redemption* song; "Emancipate yourselves from mental slavery; none but ourselves can free our mind." Together, let us help make Jamaica one of the most desirable places on the planet.

ANSWERS

POLITICS

1. ORETTE BRUCE GOLDING
2. FLORIZEL AUGUSTUS GLASSPOLE
3. HOWARD FELIX COOKE
4. ANDREW HOLNESS
5. MICHAEL MANLEY
6. PERCIVAL JAMES PATTERSON
7. EDWARD SEAGA
8. KENNETH O. HALL
9. PORTIA SIMPSON
10. PATRICK LINTON ALLEN
11. ALEXANDER BUSTAMANTE
12. LISA HANNA
13. HUGH LAWSON SHEARER
14. DONALD SANGSTER
15. ROSE LEON

SPORTS

1. COURTNEY WALSH
2. USAIN BOLT
3. DONALD QUARRIE
4. SHELLY-ANN FRASER
5. MERLENE OTTEY
6. TREVOR BERBICK
7. DAVID WELLER
8. RICHARD RUSELL
9. YOHAN BLAKE

MUSIC & ENTERTAINMENT

1. BOB MARLEY
2. MILLIE SMALL
3. FREDERICK "TOOTS" HIBBERT with TOOTS and the MAYTALS
4. ZIGGY MARLEY
5. SONNY BRADSHAW
6. JIMMY CLIFF
7. DENNIS BROWN
8. JUDY MOWATT
9. BYRON LEE

THEATRE & ART

1. CHARLES HYATT
2. MALLICA 'KAPO' REYNOLDS
3. EDNA MANLEY
4. LOUISE BENNETT-COVERLEY, AKA MISS LOU
5. OLIVER SAMUELS
6. LEONIE FORBES
7. REX NETTLEFORD
8. TREVOR RHONE
9. RANDOLPH SAMUEL WILLIAMS (MAS RON)
10. BARRINGTON WATSON

MEDIA

1. IAN BOYNE
2. BEVELEY ANDERSON DUNCAN
3. WINSTON BARNES
4. CLINT O'NEIL

EDUCATION & LITERARY

1. JOYCE LILIETH ROBINSON
2. MERVYN MORRIS
3. ERROL MORRISON
4. DOUGLAS WREXHAM ERIC FORREST
5. FAY SAUNDERS

6. KENNETH EVERALD INGRAM

7. MAUREEN CLARE and MARY DAVIES

8. ERROL MILLER

9. EDWIN ALLEN

RELIGION & HUMANITARIAN

1. GLADYS MAUD BUSTAMANTE

2. SAMUEL CARTER

3. GERRY GALLIMORE

BUSINESS-TOURISM-LAW

1. GORDON 'BUTCH' STEWART

2. JOHN LYNCH

3. LASCELLES CHIN

4. AUDREY MARKS

5. LOWELL HAWTHORNE of GOLDEN KRUST CARIBBEAN BAKERY & GRILL.

6. ERIC ANTHONY ABRAHAM

7. EDWARD ZACCA

BEAUTY & FASHION

1. CAROLE CRAWFORD

2. YENDI PHILLIPS

3. PATSY YUEN

4. CINDY BREAKSPEARE

5. LISA HANNA

6. FLOSSIE THOMAS-McNALLY

7. ANNIE LOPEZ

8. IVY RALPH

AVIATION & AGRICULTURE

1. BARRINGTON IRVING

2. MARIA ZIADIE-HADDAD

3. THOMAS PHILLIP LECKY

WHAT TOWN OR PLACE AM I?

1. SPANISH TOWN

2. PORT ROYAL

3. DEVON HOUSE-KINGSTON

4. UNIVERSITY OF THE WEST INDIES

5. BROWNS TOWN

6. BULL BAY

7. GREEN GROTTO CAVES

8. LOVERS LEAP

9. MILK RIVER BATH

10. NEW KINGSTON

11. MORANT POINT LIGHTHOUSE

12. LIME CAY

13. MANDEVILLE

14. PORT MARIA

15. PARADE

16. OLD HARBOUR

17. PORT ANTONIO

18. FALMOUTH

19. YALLAHS

20. BOG WALK

21. LACOVIA

22. SHOOTERS HILL

23. ST. ANN'S BAY

24. HELLSHIRE

25. DUNNS RIVER FALLS

26. CASTLETON

There's no doubt that for a relatively small and young nation, hundreds of Jamaicans have contributed in major ways to various areas of the society. Naturally all these Jamaicans could not be mentioned in this publication, and some readers may be understandably disappointed that some of their favorite people have not been mentioned herein. However, we pay tribute to all Jamaicans, past and present, in Jamaica or its Diaspora, who excelled, or who in one way or another contributed to making Jamaica a phenomenal nation, underlying the truth that the nation is "little but powerful" or in Jamaican dialect "wi likkle, but wi tallawah."

www.ingramcontent.com/pod-product-compliance
Lightning Source LLC
La Vergne TN
LVHW021504080426
835509LV00018B/2388